THE COMPLETE JUICING RECIPE BOOK

THE COMPLETE
JUICING
RECIPE BOOK

360 EASY RECIPES FOR A HEALTHIER LIFE

STEPHANIE LEACH, HC, CJT

PHOTOGRAPHY BY LAUREN VOLO

callisto
publishing
an imprint of Sourcebooks

Copyright © 2020 by Callisto Publishing LLC
Cover and internal design © 2020 by Callisto Publishing LLC
Photography © 2020 Lauren Volo.
Food styling by Jozeph Herceg.
Interior and Cover Designer: Michael Patti
Art Producer: Janice Ackerman
Editor: Rebecca Markley
Production Editor: Emily Sheehan

Published by Callisto Publishing LLC C/O Sourcebooks LLC
P.O. Box 4410, Naperville, Illinois 60567-4410
(630) 961-3900
callistopublishing.com

Printed and bound in China
OGP 2

THIS BOOK IS DEDICATED TO
MY HUSBAND, DOYLE,
WHO HAS ALWAYS ENCOURAGED
ME TO PURSUE MY
PASSIONS AND NEVER GIVE
UP ON MY DREAMS.

CONTENTS

INTRODUCTION

JUICING IS A POWERFUL, effective tool for creating a strong and healthy mind and body. As a certified health coach and Juice Guru certified juice therapist, I've witnessed its transformative power in myself and my clients.

By my early 40s, I was frequently tired for no discernable reason. I had packed on some unwanted pounds. I wasn't happy with my skin, and I was frustrated by chronic digestive complaints. Although many people accept extra weight and a growing list of health problems as an inevitable part of growing older, I wanted more. I wanted an energized and healthy mind and body, one that would serve me well into my 50s, 60s, and beyond.

Juicing was the answer! By drinking nutrient-rich and delicious fresh juices, combined with a diet centered on whole plant foods, I quickly reached and *maintained* my goal weight. My skin problem "mysteriously" cleared up. My digestion improved. I had energy and focus instead of afternoon slumps. After a while, I realized that I rarely got sick anymore, and if I did catch a cold, I recovered quickly.

I continue to drink a fresh juice most days, and I encourage my clients to do the same. In my experience, those who embrace daily juicing have the most success in achieving and sustaining their health goals. Starting the day with a juice floods the cells with the vitamins, minerals, and phytonutrients the body craves. Juice is concentrated nutrition, and the body knows just what to do with it. The result is true health from the inside out.

If you have a health condition, be sure to discuss any major dietary changes with your doctor, especially if you are on medication. Fueling your body with plants, including fresh juices, can result in rapid health improvements. Your doctor may need to monitor you and adjust or even eliminate certain medications.

Ready to get started? Turn the page and let your juicing journey to a healthier life begin.

PART I

THE GROUNDWORK

SUMMERTIME WATERMELON
AND SWEET PEPPER SIPPER,
PAGE 50

CHAPTER 1

JUICING BASICS

This book is full of the information you'll need to make delicious fresh juices with confidence. To get started, I'll cover what juicing is and how it differs from making smoothies. I'll share how and why fresh juices promote health and how to safely incorporate juicing into your life. You'll also find a useful section on different styles of juicing machines and how to select one that is right for you. Finally, I'll tell you how to prepare produce to make juices with maximum nutrition and flavor.

WHAT IS JUICING?

Juicing is the process of extracting the liquid from fruits and vegetables by removing the insoluble fiber with a juicing machine. The liquid, or juice, contains the water, vitamins, minerals, enzymes, and phytonutrients that are so valuable in raw plant foods. Essentially, the juicing machine does what a properly functioning digestive system would normally do: break down the cell walls of plants and liberate the nutrition. Because juice is predigested, your body can put those nutrients to work in as little as 15 to 20 minutes.

While juicing does remove most of the insoluble fiber, the *soluble* fiber remains in the juice, so you'll still enjoy its benefits: lower cholesterol, blood sugar regulation, diabetes protection, and weight loss. (Insoluble fiber is important, but the fruits and vegetables most popular for juicing have a high water content and are not the best sources of insoluble fiber anyway. By eating meals that include true high-fiber foods like beans, lentils, chickpeas, and whole grains, along with raw or cooked vegetables, you'll get the insoluble fiber you need for healthy digestion.) So, don't worry—juicing doesn't take away nutrition from your diet but greatly increases your intake of disease-fighting nutrition with every glass.

WHY JUICE?

The benefits of fresh juice are abundant. Some people turn to juicing to increase the amount and variety of vitamins, minerals, and phytonutrients in their diets and to improve their overall health. Others start juicing for more specific reasons, such as to improve their brain, heart, or bone health, resolve digestive complaints, boost their immune system, cleanse and detoxify their bodies, or build strong bones.

General Health

Just one glass of freshly pressed juice each day provides more nutrition than most people get all week! In a 2017 meta-analysis of 95 studies that included more than two million people, researchers concluded that 10 servings of fruits and vegetables per day are needed for maximum protection from health issues like heart disease, cardiovascular disease, stroke, type 2 diabetes, cancer, and premature death. That's about 1¾ pounds of produce. Unfortunately, most people in the United States eat less than a cup of fruit and only about 1½ cups of vegetables per day. Since one 16-ounce juice could easily contain two pounds of produce, juicing makes it easy to maximize the health benefits of fruits and vegetables.

Brain Health

Micronutrients called polyphenols are found in many fruits and vegetables and have powerful antioxidant properties that can help protect against Alzheimer's disease and dementia. In a study of more than 1,800 people, drinking polyphenol-rich fruit and vegetable juices three or more times per week was associated with a substantially decreased risk of Alzheimer's disease. Furthermore, another study shows that quercetin, a type of polyphenol, can cross the blood-brain barrier and reduce brain cancer cells' ability to multiply.

Cleansing and Detoxifying

Detoxification occurs on a cellular level. Cruciferous vegetables are rich in sulfur compounds that the body converts to isothiocyanates (ITCs), and orange, yellow, and green vegetables are high in beneficial pigments called carotenoids. When you juice these vegetables, you drive enzyme production that will help your body excrete carcinogens and heavy metals. Additionally, when you drink juice instead of eating raw foods, your body remains in a fasting state and can focus more energy on toxin removal.

Digestion

According to a recent survey by the National Institute of Diabetes and Digestive and Kidney Diseases, 60 to 70 million Americans are living with digestive complaints, such as gas, bloating, and abdominal pain. Juicing can help! Certain fruits and vegetables are especially useful to relieve constipation and bloating, reduce acid reflux, lower inflammation, and soothe irritated bowels. Drinking freshly pressed juice can even help rebuild intestinal walls and repair a leaky gut.

Heart Health (or Cardiovascular Health)

Available research proves that juicing can help you reduce your LDL cholesterol and triglycerides and raise beneficial HDL. The phytonutrients in fresh juice promote cardiovascular health by providing powerful antioxidants and anti-inflammatory nutrients to prevent the oxidation of LDL and help reduce the damage it causes. Juices can also help lower blood pressure naturally, an important factor in heart health.

Immune System

Fresh juice provides your body with energy, as well as the vitamins and micronutrients essential for healthy immune function, such as zinc, selenium, iron, copper, folate, and vitamins A, B_6, C, and E. A single 16-ounce juice combination of carrot, yellow bell pepper, and parsley delivers more than twice the daily recommended amounts of vitamins A and C, as well as a substantial amount of vitamin B_6, which plays a vital role in immune cell proliferation and antibody production.

Blood and Bone Health

Calcium, iron, zinc, manganese, folate, boron, and vitamins B_6, B_9, B_{12}, and K are just a few of the nutrients necessary for building strong bones and healthy blood. Fortunately, these are found in abundance—and in an easy-to-assimilate form—in fresh juices, especially greens. Adding broccoli, Brussels sprouts, collards, kale, mustard greens, Swiss chard, and other greens to your juice blends provides calcium that is easy to absorb.

Mental Health

Fresh juices can ease the symptoms of depression and help lift your mood and energy. Juices provide a quick and healthy energy boost, which can help you feel like doing more. Certain juice combinations can deliver high amounts of folate and vitamins C and K, which have been shown to help alleviate depression.

JUICE WITH CARE

Juicing is an effective way to increase the nutrition in your diet and foster healthier choices. But it's not a magic bullet. When I started juicing in my 20s, I didn't give up my pizza-and-burger lifestyle, so my juicing results were limited. It wasn't until I was willing to make other dietary changes that I experienced the full benefits of juicing, including a healthy weight. It's our overall dietary pattern that influences our health. For maximum health benefits, including an ideal weight and chronic disease prevention and reversal, I encourage you to combine juicing with a diet centered on whole plant foods. You'll feel amazing!

Almost anyone can safely add fresh juices to their diet, including children, the elderly, and women who are pregnant. Here are some recommendations for safe juicing, including some areas where you may need to exercise caution.

1. If you are on medications or have a serious health condition, please consult with your doctor about

any major changes to your diet. Read the package inserts that come with your medications. They will often list any foods that can interfere with the medicines you are taking.

2. Juicing and eating healthier plant foods can result in rapid health improvements! If you are on blood pressure or diabetes medication, it may need to be adjusted rather quickly. If you are on a blood thinning medication, work with your doctor to adjust your medication to match your new daily vitamin K intake from dark leafy greens.

3. Juice a variety of vegetables and rotate your greens. People tend to get into trouble when they juice enormous amounts of a cruciferous vegetable over an extended period.

4. If you have recently been taking antibiotics or have a long history of taking antibiotics, your gut flora, responsible for metabolizing a compound called oxalate found in many foods, has been compromised. Consuming too many oxalates while in this condition could lead to kidney stone formation, so avoid juicing

large amounts of high-oxalate produce like spinach, kale, beet greens, beets, and Swiss chard. Likewise, if you have kidney disease or gout, you may want to swap high-oxalate produce for low-oxalate options like bok choy and romaine. (For most people, juicing dark leafy greens isn't a problem and shouldn't be avoided.)

5. If you are concerned about kidney stones, the best way to avoid them is to greatly reduce all animal protein and salt and adopt a high-fiber diet that's rich in fruits and vegetables. You can also add lemon or lime to your juices because the citrates bind with calcium in place of oxalates, reducing the risk of high levels of calcium oxalate in the urine, which can lead to kidney stone formation.

6. If you are diabetic or have unstable blood sugar, you may want to limit the amount of fruit in your juices and avoid moderate and high glycemic index juices like watermelon, pineapple, and cantaloupe. Monitor your blood glucose and consult with your doctor if you intend to drink

fruit-heavy juices. Fortunately, the polyphenols in juice from apples, strawberries, and grapes have been shown to help regulate blood sugar levels.

7. Pregnant women should avoid juicing large amounts of parsley because it can induce contractions. Additionally, when pregnant or breastfeeding, you should not start a juice fast because it may cause toxins to be released to the baby, either in the womb or through breast milk. However, adding a juice or two to your diet each day will increase your nutrition and hydration.

JUICES VS. SMOOTHIES

Juices are made in a juicing machine that removes the insoluble fiber. Smoothies are made in a blender where the insoluble fiber is blended up with the rest of the food. Even if the resulting drink is a liquid that looks like a juice, a drink made in a blender is not a true juice because it contains insoluble fiber.

There are benefits to both juicing and blending. Each have their own place in a healthy diet. Smoothies are usually made with fruit suitable for a smoothie and a few servings of vegetables at most. Liquid is often added to the blender to help blend up the produce. Protein powders, nut butters, and seeds can be added for more nutrition. Smoothies are fast and convenient portable meals.

You won't find bananas, nut butters, or many other popular smoothie ingredients in a juice. Because the fiber is removed, a 16-ounce glass of juice can contain the nutrition of a dozen or more servings of produce. If you tried to blend a pound of carrots, an apple, and half a bunch of kale, the resulting drink would be totally unpalatable. But juice those ingredients and you get a smooth, delicious beverage rich in nutrients. Because no water or other liquid is added to juice, the nutrition density is about 2.5:1 compared to a smoothie.

HOW TO GET STARTED

If you're new to juicing, this section will help answer some of the questions you may have about what juicer to buy and how to prepare fruits and vegetables for juicing.

Selecting a Juicer

With so many choices available, you may be wondering which juicing machine is the best. The answer depends on your budget, how often you will be making juice, the amount of juice you will be making, the counter space you have available, and the kinds of fruits and vegetables you'll be juicing.

Centrifugal Juicers

This style of juicer uses tiny teeth on a metal basket that spins at high revolutions per minute (rpms) to shred the produce. Centrifugal juicers are fast, are affordable, and handle hard fruits and vegetables well. The downside of this style of juicer is that it whips air into the juice, which speeds oxidation. Juices made with centrifugal juicers should be consumed immediately. The pulp is generally wetter, so the yield of juice is lower than other styles.

Single-Auger Juicers

Also known as a slow juicer, a single-auger juicer is an upright or horizontal machine with an auger that turns at low rpms to gently crush the produce. The result is a more stable juice that can be stored for a day or two under the proper conditions (see How to Store Your Juice, page 11). They are self-feeding, which allows you to start juicing while continuing to prep produce. This kind of juicer does a good job on soft and hard fruits and vegetables, as well as leafy greens. The pulp will be more dry than with a centrifugal juicer, which means a greater yield of juice in your glass.

Triturating Juicers

Triturating juicers (also called twin-gear juicers or double-auger juicers) utilize twin gears that crush and grind the produce into small particles for maximum nutrient extraction and yield. They are excellent machines for hard or stringy produce and leafy greens. You won't have to chop your celery or kale with this kind of juicer. The only downside is that it doesn't handle soft fruit or produce that tends to foam, like pineapple, as well as a single-auger juicer does. If you want to juice wheatgrass and primarily leafy greens and hard produce, and you don't mind pushing the produce through, this may be the juicer for you.

Produce Procedure

The quality of your juice depends on the quality of your produce. Certified organic or biodynamically grown fruits and vegetables are best. The age of your produce, how it's been stored, and how you prep your produce for juicing will influence the overall healthiness and nutritional value of your juice.

When to Buy

Fruits and vegetables harvested at or close to their peak ripeness will have the most flavor and nutrition. Most grocery stores have a mix of produce grown nearby or in the region, as well as produce trucked in from across the country or shipped in from around the world. To maximize nutrition and flavor and reduce cost, make good use of locally grown or seasonal produce. If you have the space available, growing your own greens allows you to pick and juice immediately.

Also consider when you will be making juice and buy fruits and vegetables that will be in good condition by the time you are turning on your juicer. Limp greens don't make good juice! Plan out your juices and buy just enough produce to prevent waste.

How to Wash

It's important to wash your produce properly to remove dirt and bacteria and reduce pesticide residues. Washing produce under running water and rubbing with your hand or a vegetable brush removes 98 percent of bacteria and 80 percent of pesticide residues. The water temperature should be as close to that of the produce you are washing as possible. If you prefer to use a vinegar-water solution, the effective formula is 1 part vinegar to 3 parts water. If you want to take a step further to remove more of the possible pesticides, you can soak hard produce in a sink filled with cold water and 4 tablespoons of baking soda (or a salad spinner–size bowl filled with water and 1 teaspoon of baking soda) for 5 to 15 minutes. After your vegetables have had their "bath," rinse them under running water, giving them a scrub. For leafy greens, a shorter soak time of 1 to 2 minutes followed by a rinse under running water will be enough. Delicate berries can be rinsed quickly with the baking soda water, then rinsed again under clean running water.

How to Prep Your Produce

Before juicing, trim off the ends of root vegetables like carrots and beets because these areas can harbor bacteria. Always remove the very outer colored part of the rind of oranges, grapefruits, and mandarins. The volatile oils in these rinds are difficult to digest. Retain as much of the white pith as possible because this area contains valuable nutrients. You can leave on the rinds of lemons and limes, although some people find lime rinds very bitter. Peeling red beets can reduce their earthy flavor and make the juice more palatable but isn't required. Remove any limp leaves and any damaged areas or bad spots on your produce.

What to Do with Pulp

You may be wondering what you could or should do with the pulp after juicing. Juice pulp can be added to baked goods and soups or dehydrated into crackers. I'll provide tips with some of the juice recipes on how you can repurpose the pulp. But if you don't have the time or desire to reuse it, don't feel guilty. Most of the nutrition has been liberated from the insoluble fiber and is in your juice glass. If you can, it's a good idea to compost the pulp or find a neighbor or farm that can compost it or use it in some way.

How to Store Your Juice

Juice made in a centrifugal juicer should be consumed immediately, or at least very soon after juicing. Centrifugal juicers whip air into the juice, speeding oxidation and the breakdown of beneficial phytonutrients.

Juice made in a single-auger juicer or a triturating juicer can generally be safely stored for 24 to 48 hours. Depending on your juicer and juicing conditions, you may be able to store a juice for up to 72 hours. Check with the manufacturer for its recommendations.

Fresh is best, but if you must store your juice, follow these guidelines:

- Oxygen is the enemy. I use canning jars with a lid and a screw band and either fill the jar to the rim or use a vacuum sealer to remove the air.
- Store your juice in the coldest part of your refrigerator. You can also place your filled juice jars in the freezer for 10 to 15 minutes to speed the cooling process before transferring them to the refrigerator. (Set a timer so you don't forget about them!)
- Add some lemon or lime to your juice blend to help maintain the freshness of your juice.

CHAPTER 2

FOODS
FOR
JUICING

The following fruits and vegetables are the most popular choices for juicing. The nutrients and health benefits that have been discovered for each one could fill pages, and research is ongoing. But here are the most notable highlights that you may find interesting and helpful as you explore your juicing options.

FRUITS

Fresh, raw fruit juice is not only delicious, but it also contains vitamins, minerals, soluble fiber, and important disease-fighting phytonutrients. In a meta-analysis of 18 randomized controlled trials, consumption of 100 percent fruit juice was not associated with an increased risk of type 2 diabetes and did not negatively affect glycemic control. You can use fruit to sweeten and bring variety to your daily vegetable juice blends and enjoy 100 percent fruit juices on occasion if your health condition allows.

Apples

Containing dozens of phytonutrients, apples provide antioxidants that protect blood vessels and the heart by reducing LDL cholesterol oxidation, which causes hardening of the arteries. Apples may also help lower total cholesterol and triglycerides. Pectin, the primary soluble fiber in apples, slows stomach emptying and helps stabilize blood sugar. Apples are also being researched for colon cancer prevention.

Blackberries

Blackberries are high in vitamin C and anthocyanins, which are important antioxidants that protect against cancer and heart disease. Blackberries are also a good source of vitamin K for proper blood clotting. In an animal study, blackberries improved cognitive function. Like most berries, blackberries are very low in sugar.

Blueberries

Like blackberries, blueberries are best known for their anthocyanins, which not only offer protection against heart disease and cancer but also boost cognitive function and memory. These powerhouse berries may also help regulate blood pressure and blood sugar. Stilbenoids, naturally occurring compounds found in blueberries, are chemoprotective, and lab studies show blueberry extracts inhibit cancer cell proliferation and induce apoptosis, or cancer cell death.

Cantaloupe

Cantaloupe is an excellent source of vitamin C and vitamin A, which provides anti-inflammatory and anti-oxidant benefits. Cantaloupe is also a good source of B vitamins, vitamin K, and several minerals including copper, magnesium, and potassium. If the melon is organic, you can juice the rind.

Cranberries

Packed full of outstanding phytonutrients, cranberry juice has been shown to raise HDL cholesterol, lower triglycerides, and reduce LDL cholesterol oxidation, lowering the risk of cardiovascular disease. This tart berry juice also lowers fasting blood sugar levels and helps increase levels of a hormone that decreases insulin resistance and fat storage. It may also help prevent or improve certain urinary tract infections.

Dragon Fruit (Pitaya, Pitahaya)

This exotic-looking tropical fruit supplies vitamins, minerals, and fiber to your diet. Dragon fruit can help boost your iron levels and strengthen your immune system. The red variety contains betalains and carotenoids that are cancer protective. You can juice the thick outer skin along with the pulp and seeds.

Grapefruit

Grapefruit juice is highly antioxidant and offers a host of health benefits. High in vitamin C, it is anti-inflammatory, helps fight colds, and can reduce the severity of asthma and arthritis. Lycopene, found in red and pink grapefruit, and other phytonutrients in this citrus fruit are anticancer. This juice can also lower LDL cholesterol and may help prevent kidney stones. Include the inner white pith where the anti-inflammatory and antioxidant flavonoid hesperidin

is found. **(Avoid grapefruit if you are taking certain statin drugs, antimicrobials, blood thinners, pain medications, or certain other medications for blood pressure, heart rhythm, or prostate issues. Check your package insert or the Drugs.com "Drug Interactions Checker" page at drugs.com/drug_interactions.html for more information on food interactions.)**

Grapes

Grape juice is anticancer, antimicrobial, anti-inflammatory, and anti-aging. The cardiovascular benefits of grapes are lengthy, including reduced LDL, better blood pressure regulation, and reduced clumping of platelets. Grapes help balance blood sugar and increase insulin sensitivity. Grape juice is also good for your brain. Look for organic red, black, or purple grapes. Grapes with seeds are even better!

Honeydew Melon

Like cantaloupe, honeydew melon is a good source of vitamin C, which is important for collagen production and a healthy immune system. Honeydew's high potassium content can help prevent hypertension and supports healthy bones. With vitamin

B_6 and folate, honeydew helps support healthy brain function.

Kiwifruit

Kiwifruit is an excellent source of vitamin C. The phytonutrients in kiwifruit protect DNA from damage, and kiwi can lower your risk of blood clots without the side effects of aspirin. Kiwifruit consumption can also lower triglycerides. Juice the whole fruit; peeling is not necessary.

Lemons

Like other citrus fruits, lemons are high in vitamin C, which helps fight free radicals. Lemons and limes contain important cancer-fighting compounds called limonoids that persist in the bloodstream many times longer than the anticancer compounds in green tea. Lemons are an important part of an anti-inflammatory diet. If your lemons are organic, juice them with their peels, which is where limonene and other beneficial flavonoids are found.

Limes

Limes are very similar to lemons in nutrition and health benefits but are slightly more acidic. The flavonol glycoside found in limes has been shown to have antibiotic effects. Although you can juice lime peels, many people find them too bitter, so you may want to peel them.

Mango

Mango is an excellent source of vitamin B_6 and a good source of vitamins A and C. High in the soluble fiber pectin, mangos can help lower cholesterol and regulate digestion. Mango peel contains a unique antioxidant called mangiferin, which has been shown in animal studies to be anticancer and supports a healthy heart by lowering cholesterol and triglycerides.

Oranges and Tangerines

Fresh orange juice is rich in vitamin C and a good source of folate, potassium, and magnesium. Orange juice consumption has been shown to lower cholesterol and blood pressure and decrease inflammation, and it may reduce the risk of kidney stones. Include the inner white pith where the anti-inflammatory and antioxidant flavonoid hesperidin is found.

Papaya

Heart-healthy papayas contain whopping amounts of vitamin C that can help boost your immunity and reduce stress hormones. They are also rich in vitamin A for eye health. Papaya contains the unique enzymes papain and chymopapain, which help reduce inflammation, improve digestion of proteins, and even relieve menstrual pain.

Passion Fruit

Fragrant, sweet, and tart passion fruit juice provides vitamins A and C, supporting your body's muscles, cartilage, blood vessels and collagen. It also supplies some iron, potassium, calcium, magnesium, and folate. Cut open this tropical fruit and scoop out the seeds and yellow flesh. Discard the peel.

Peaches and Nectarines

Peaches and nectarines are good sources of vitamins A and C, which are great for immunity and skin health. These stone fruits may reduce LDL, or "bad," cholesterol and help regulate blood pressure. Compounds in peaches and nectarines may improve skin hydration, reduce allergy symptoms, and even kill cancerous cells. Select firm, ripe peaches or nectarines for the most antioxidant activity.

Pears

The flavonols in pears help improve insulin sensitivity. In studies, the phytonutrients in pears have been shown to reduce the risk of certain cancers, including gastric and esophageal cancers. Pears improve digestion and are considered a low-allergy food. Red pears contain anthocyanins in their skins and are good for heart health.

Pineapple

Packed with vitamin C and manganese, pineapple juice is highly antioxidant and supports energy production in cells. Bromelain, found in the core, is a unique mixture of nutrients that is anti-inflammatory, improving osteoarthritis and reducing pain and swelling after surgery and strenuous exercise. Bromelain also improves digestion and has been shown in studies to be potentially anticancer.

Plums

Plums contain unique phenols that neutralize a particularly dangerous free radical that can damage healthy cells. They also prevent oxygen damage to fats, including brain cells. Plum juice contains soluble fiber that helps lower cholesterol and promote the growth of healthy bacteria in the gut.

Pomegranate

The juice of the ruby red arils inside a pomegranate has been shown to lower systolic blood pressure by about five points. It may also help keep carotid arteries clear and improve blood flow to the heart. This juice can help you maintain a healthy weight and may slow the progression of prostate cancer. **Never juice the root, stem, or peel of a pomegranate because they contain poisons.**

Pomelo (Pummelo)

Pomelo juice is nutritionally similar to grapefruit but isn't as tart. It's high in vitamin C, with one fruit supplying 600 percent of the recommended daily amount. It also supplies 37 percent of your daily potassium needs for good blood circulation. Include the inner white pith where the anti-inflammatory and antioxidant flavonoid hesperidin is found.

Raspberries

This berry supplies high amounts of vitamin C, manganese, and fiber. Raspberries contain anthocyanins, which can help improve insulin and blood sugar balance. Raspberries are also anticancer and good for the brain. Look for ripe, organic berries for the greatest antioxidant benefits.

Strawberries

This popular berry can help regulate insulin and balance blood sugar. Strawberry intake is associated with delaying cognitive decline in older adults by up to 2 ½ years. Because they are very high in vitamin C and other antioxidants, strawberries are anticancer, anti-inflammatory, and good for heart health.

Watermelon

Watermelon has more lycopene than tomatoes and is more easily absorbed. Watermelon is good for your heart and produces nitric oxide to fuel your performance in endurance sports. Researchers have found that watermelon juice can lower your risk of high blood pressure. Watermelon is also anti-inflammatory and antioxidant. The seeds are highly nutritious.

VEGETABLES

While many people find it easy to eat fruit, they may not be eating enough vegetables. Fortunately, vegetable juices deliver mind-blowing amounts of nutrition in just a few sips. Juicing dark leafy greens, as well as cruciferous and root vegetables, is without a doubt one of the best ways to ensure a healthy life. I encourage you to make daily vegetable-heavy juices the cornerstone of your healthy eating habits.

Arugula

This leafy green belongs to the cancer-fighting brassica family that includes broccoli and cabbage. Arugula is high in minerals, making it a good choice for bone health. This slightly bitter or peppery-tasting green supports detoxification and is best juiced along with other greens and vegetables.

Asparagus

Asparagus is an excellent source of vitamins B_1, B_2, C, E, and K, as well as many minerals including folate, copper, and selenium. Asparagus is an important source of quercetin, a well-studied polyphenol that supports brain and cardiovascular health. This vegetable also contains common plant-based compounds called saponins that are anticancer. Asparagus is a natural diuretic and could irritate the kidneys in large amounts.

Beets

Beets are powerful cleansers and should be used moderately in combination with other fruits and vegetables. Both red and gold beets are detoxifying and blood building. Beets are rich in nitrates, which your body converts to nitric oxide, improving blood flow and boosting stamina.

Bell Peppers

Red, yellow, and orange bell peppers are the best vegetable sources of vitamin C and good sources of a wide range of other vitamins and minerals for heart health, weight management, and balanced blood sugar. They're also high in carotenoids that support eye, brain, and heart health.

Bok Choy

This cruciferous, cancer-fighting vegetable is easy on the palate and an excellent choice for juicing because its crunchy white or light green stalks are high in water. It contains more than 70 antioxidants, and it is anticancer and a good source of anti-inflammatory omega-3 fatty acids and vitamin K for blood and bone health.

Broccoli

Like other cruciferous vegetables, this highly studied anticancer food is anti-inflammatory and enhances detoxification. Some of its beneficial nutrients are damaged by heat, making it a good choice for juicing. Broccoli consumption is associated with lower LDL cholesterol, and it contains the antioxidants lutein and zeaxanthin for eye health.

Cabbage

Cabbage is anti-inflammatory and anticancer. Cabbage juice can help prevent and heal peptic ulcers and can help relieve ulcerative colitis symptoms. Red or purple cabbage provides anthocyanins for heart health and red blood cell protection, as well as polyphenols that promote brain health.

Carrots

In a large-scale 10-year study, carrots were associated with significantly lower cardiovascular disease risk. Carrots contain falcarinol, which is anticancer. Studies also support carrots for eye health and liver health. Beta-carotene, the most prominent antioxidant in carrots, helps boost immunity and is beneficial to overall good health. Red and purple carrots provide anthocyanins.

Cauliflower

This white cruciferous vegetable is surprisingly high in vitamin C. Cauliflower and other cruciferous vegetables aid detoxification and support the body's immune, cardiovascular, and digestive systems. Cauliflower is also highly antioxidant.

Celery

Celery juice contains antioxidant and anti-inflammatory nutrients that support the lining of the stomach and decrease the risk of gastric ulcers. Celery also contains powerful anti-cancer compounds. Celery provides vitamins, natural electrolytes, phenolic compounds, and other nutrients. You don't have to drink it plain to gain the benefits.

Collards

Collard greens are a cruciferous vegetable offering cancer protection benefits due to their sulfur-containing compounds called glucosinolates. Collards also support cardiovascular health and a healthy digestive tract. This juice is strong-tasting, and one small leaf is enough to include in a juice to get the benefits.

Cucumbers

This high-volume juicing vegetable contains at least 73 different compounds that provide antioxidant and anti-inflammatory support. Polyphenols called lignans in cucumbers decrease the risk of estrogen-related cancers. Cucumber juice is also great for the skin.

Dandelion

Dandelion greens are full of vitamin K for bone and brain health. This often-overlooked herb is also a good source of vitamin A for healthy skin and eyes. Dandelion is high in soluble fiber to support heart health, weight management, and healthy gut flora. It also has a protective effect on the liver.

Fennel

Slightly sweet fennel juice contains a unique array of phytonutrients, including a compound called anethole that is anti-inflammatory and anti-cancer. Fennel is also a good source of vitamin C, folate, and minerals.

Kale

Kale juice has been proven to lower LDL cholesterol, raise beneficial HDL cholesterol, and improve other cardiovascular health markers. This anti-inflammatory, antioxidant-rich, cruciferous leafy green helps with detoxification and cancer prevention.

It's also the top lutein-containing food for eye health and the top source of vitamin K for healthy bones and blood.

Kohlrabi

This brassica family vegetable, related to cabbage, is anticancer and has more vitamin C than an orange. Kohlrabi is good for your overall health and promotes strong bones, a healthy weight, and good vision, digestion, and blood pressure. Kohlrabi juice has a strong flavor, so it's best to combine it with other vegetables.

Mustard Greens

Pungent mustard greens are in the cruciferous family and provide anticancer, anti-inflammatory, and detoxification support. These greens are from the mustard plant, so their juice is warming and can improve circulation and relieve congestion. Mustard greens are a good source of vitamins K, A, and E, as well as calcium and iron. Start with one small leaf in a juice blend.

Radish

Radish juice is high in vitamin C and is a good source of vitamin B_6, potassium, folate, iron, and minerals. Radishes are traditionally used to treat asthma, jaundice, inflammation in the bladder, and kidney stones. They're also used as a diuretic, laxative, and blood purifier. Radishes are from the cruciferous family, and their sulfur compounds are anticancer and support detoxification.

Romaine

This lettuce is high in nutrition as well as water, making it an excellent choice for juice. Romaine provides vitamin C and beta-carotene to help prevent LDL oxidation. Its potassium and folic acid also support cardiovascular health. Look for large, heavy heads of romaine with dark outer leaves.

Spinach

Spinach is the vegetable richest in chlorophyll, which helps delay stomach emptying, decrease hunger hormones, and increase satiety hormones, making it an excellent choice for weight loss or maintenance. Spinach is also an outstanding source of magnesium, iron, calcium, folate, and other vitamins.

Sweet Potato

The proteins in sweet potatoes have been shown to suppress the growth of leukemia cells and colon cancer cells in a petri dish. Sweet potatoes are anti-inflammatory. They benefit the brain and nerves and help regulate blood sugar.

Swiss Chard

Chard is high in vitamins K, A, and C. It is an excellent source of minerals and a good source of calcium. This leafy green is good for blood sugar regulation due to its array of B vitamins. Chard is good for cardiovascular health as it can help regulate blood pressure and reduce total and LDL cholesterol. Chard with colored stems provides anticancer and neuroprotective properties.

Tomato

Containing lycopene and other antioxidants, tomatoes are best known for their cardiovascular benefits, including the ability to lower cholesterol and triglycerides and reduce the damage to healthy fats in the bloodstream. Tomatoes help lower the risk of prostate cancer in men and may reduce the risk of nonmelanoma skin cancer.

Winter Squash

The orange flesh of most winter squash, like butternut and pumpkin, provide an array of anti-inflammatory carotenoids. Winter squash is also high in pectin, which helps regulate blood sugar and helps you feel fuller longer. This food group boosts your intake of almost every major category of nutrients.

Zucchini

Summer squash like zucchini are good sources of minerals and B vitamins. Zucchini juice is cooling to the body and a natural colon cleanser. The flavor is bland, making it a good addition to juice blends with carrots or stronger-tasting greens.

HERBS, SPICES, AND MIX-INS

Apple Cider Vinegar

Organic, unfiltered apple cider vinegar has been proven to reduce fasting blood sugar better than antidiabetic drugs and to reduce blood sugar spikes from high glycemic meals by 23 percent. Vinegar has also been shown to support weight loss. Adding a couple of teaspoons to your juice can help you get to the optimal daily dose of two tablespoons, spread throughout the day.

Chia Seeds

Chia seeds are an excellent source of omega-3 fatty acids and a good source of plant protein, fiber, minerals, and antioxidants. When added to juice or water, the seeds swell and form a gel. Adding chia seeds to your juice will slow the rate of absorption and slow down detoxification on a juice fast if needed. They may also help improve satiety and reduce the number of calories you consume at a future meal.

Cilantro

This leafy green herb is regarded as a detoxifier, helping your cells release heavy metals. When combined with a chelator like the algae chlorella, your body can more efficiently expel those metal toxins. Cilantro is also antibacterial, anti-inflammatory, and antidiabetic. It may help lower blood sugar, lower LDL cholesterol, and increase good HDL cholesterol. Limit cilantro juice to one ounce mixed into a juice blend.

Cinnamon

This warming and pleasant spice is anti-inflammatory, antibacterial, and antimicrobial. Cinnamon slows the rate of stomach emptying, reduces blood sugar spikes, and improves insulin sensitivity. The scent of this spice boosts brain activity. Ground cinnamon is especially tasty in apple, winter squash, and root vegetable juices.

Coconut Water

Coconut water from fresh, young Thai coconuts is a delicious tropical addition to your juices. Coconut water is hydrating, provides electrolytes and potassium, and cleanses the digestive tract. In animal studies, coconut water

improved blood sugar control and lowered cholesterol.

Garlic

Garlic is a natural antibiotic and is useful during cold and flu season to combat infections, expel phlegm, and alleviate congestion in the sinuses and lungs. Garlic is also anticancer and good for heart health. Juice the garlic first and follow with other vegetables, especially greens, to help remove the odor and flavor from your machine.

Ginger Root

Spicy and warming ginger juice is an effective expectorant, immunity booster, and digestive aid. It can relieve nausea, dizziness, and vomiting. Ginger is a powerful anti-inflammatory juice ingredient, relieving pain and swelling associated with osteoarthritis and rheumatoid arthritis. It is anticancer according to studies on gastrointestinal and ovarian cancer cells. Start with a ½- to 1-inch piece. You do not need to peel it.

Parsley

The juice of this herb is highly beneficial for the thyroid, adrenals, eyes, and urinary tract. It strengthens and cleanses the bladder and kidneys. Like cilantro, parsley helps your body get rid of heavy metals and chemical toxins. It's good for upper respiratory congestion and infections. Because parsley is so strong, never drink it alone in amounts greater than an ounce or two. Preferably, drink it in a juice blend.

Superfood Powders

Green superfood powders include algae, like spirulina and chlorella, and dehydrated grass juices, like wheatgrass, alfalfa, and barley. Berry superfood powders include acai, goji, camu camu, and maqui. These powders make it easy to boost your juice to the next level by adding highly antioxidant and phytonutrient-rich foods that are difficult or impossible to juice with a home machine. Read the ingredient lists and choose an organic brand without added sweeteners or fillers.

Turmeric Root

The research on turmeric proves it to be anti-inflammatory, detoxifying, anticancer, blood sugar balancing, brain boosting, and heart healthy. The pigments in turmeric will permanently stain, so do not let turmeric juice sit on your countertop. Juice a 1-inch piece first and follow with the rest of your ingredients to help remove the staining oils from your machine. Add a pinch of black pepper to your turmeric juice blends to increase the absorption of curcumin, the main active compound in turmeric.

FAQS

What is the best way to incorporate juicing into my diet, and how much juice should I drink?

I recommend enjoying a 16- to 32-ounce juice first thing in the morning on an empty stomach and waiting 20 minutes before eating anything. Sip it slowly and notice the sustained energy you get without the caffeine. You can also flip this and enjoy your juice at dinnertime. Drinking a juice in the morning or evening in place of a meal is an effective form of intermittent fasting. The juice gives you some energy, along with exceptional nutrition, which staves off hunger while extending your fasting window. Fresh juice is a fantastic way to power your workout or rehydrate. Enjoy a juice as a healthy, energizing afternoon snack. Doing a seasonal juice fast or a juice and raw food cleanse and detox three to four times per year is also beneficial and highly recommended. (Visit StephanieLeach.com to see when my next group juice cleanse is scheduled.)

I am very busy and don't have much time to make juice. Any tips?

First, I would recommend investing in a single-auger or triturating juicer. Juice made with these kinds of juicers lasts longer (when stored properly), allowing you to make juice every other day or even every three days. Second, prep your produce when you bring it home. Wash your greens and spin them dry. Wash and scrub celery, cucumbers, peppers, carrots, and apples. (Do not wash berries in advance.) To minimize oxidation and loss of nutrients, reserve most of the cutting or chopping for juicing day. You can also place the ingredients needed for each juice you plan to make during the week into separate reusable produce bags or containers to make daily juicing faster and easier.

Does fresh juice contain protein?

Yes! Proteins are made of chains of amino acids, and **all plant foods contain all the essential amino acids** that must be obtained from our diet. The juice from one bunch of kale provides about 10 grams of protein, and the juice from 12 medium asparagus spears has almost 3 grams of protein. There is no need to combine certain foods to create "complete" proteins. Your body is smart! It recycles amino acids and combines them with new ones to synthesize proteins as needed.

Doesn't juice have too much sugar?

Raw, fresh juice from your juicing machine is not the same as filtered, heat-pasteurized juices sold in grocery stores that have little nutritional value left. Juice made at home contains polyphenols and soluble fiber (and even a small amount of insoluble fiber), and your body processes it differently. The sugar in fresh juice is not the same as table sugar. For instance, apples, berries, and grapes contain polyphenols that protect you from blood sugar spikes. Cloudy apple juice, the kind you get from your juicer, has about the same glycemic load as eating a whole apple. Additionally, you can control how much fruit or root vegetables go into your juice blend if you have a health condition that requires you to limit the fructose in your juice.

I have a centrifugal juicer. How can I get the most yield out of my produce?

For leafy greens, roll them up or ball them up and put them through the juicer sandwiched between two pieces of hard vegetables or apple. This will extend the contact time with the blades and improve yield. If your juice pulp is wet, you can run it back through the juicer to extract more nutrition and liquid. You might need to put the juice through a fine mesh strainer to remove the extra fiber that makes it into your glass.

Help! My juice tastes too bitter/ sweet/boring. What can I do?

You can likely salvage it and make it drinkable. If your juice is too bitter, you can add more cucumber or celery to dilute the bitter ingredients and add some apple for sweetness. If your juice is too sweet for your liking, add some lemon, lime, or kiwifruit. If it tastes flat and boring, it probably has too much of a bland base ingredient (like cucumber). Add some dark leafy greens, carrots, or lemon to give it more body and flavor.

ABOUT THE RECIPES

These recipes are tested, nutrient-rich combinations of fruits and vegetables that will help you reach your health goals. I have also made every effort to make them drinkable and delicious! If you are new to juicing, you may want to start with some of the more fruit-forward juices and gradually move to the more vegetable- and greens-heavy juices as your palate adjusts. The recipes often end with a fruit or vegetable with a high water content to help wash any remaining nutrients from the previous produce into your juice glass. Most of the recipes yield about 16 ounces, which is a convenient canning jar size for storage, but yields will vary depending on your produce and juicer. I've also included tips on ways you can use the pulp from some recipes, as well as other produce tips and suggestions for optional add-ins.

PART II

THE RECIPES

SWEET POTATO PIE,
PAGE 41

CHAPTER 3

BRAIN
HEALTH

What we eat and drink affects every part of our body, including how our brain functions. The recipes in this section feature berries that improve memory, coordination, and mood. There is strong evidence that berries may help prevent age-related memory loss. Berries and other colorful vegetables like carrots and orange, red, and yellow bell peppers are high in antioxidants, countering oxidative stress on the brain, which may lower your risk of neurodegenerative diseases.

Cruciferous vegetables are included for their glucosinolates, or sulfur-containing compounds, that the body converts to isothiocyanates (ITCs) that may also help prevent or slow dementia, Alzheimer's disease, and Parkinson's disease. In older adults, beets have been shown to improve blood flow to the frontal lobe, the part of the brain responsible for important cognitive skills. The betaine in beets supports dopamine and serotonin levels for good mental health. You'll also see the spice cinnamon for its positive effect on mood, memory, and concentration, as well as ginger and turmeric root for their anti-inflammatory effects on the brain.

STRAWBERRY TEASER

MAKES ABOUT 16 OUNCES

BRAIN HEALTH, DIGESTION SUPPORT, HEART HEALTH, IMMUNE SUPPORT, MOOD LIFTER, WEIGHT LOSS

1 cup strawberries
3 large celery stalks
Handful spinach
1 medium apple
½ lemon
1 large cucumber

Juice the strawberries first, then alternate the remaining ingredients, finishing with the cucumber.

EASY CITRUS SPINACH

MAKES ABOUT 16 OUNCES

BRAIN HEALTH, DIGESTION SUPPORT, HEART HEALTH, IMMUNE SUPPORT, MOOD LIFTER, WEIGHT LOSS

1 large celery stalk
Handful spinach
1 large pink or red grapefruit, peeled
3 small oranges, peeled

Alternate ingredients, finishing with the orange or the grapefruit.

SWEET DREAMS

MAKES ABOUT 16 OUNCES

BRAIN HEALTH, DIGESTION SUPPORT, HEART HEALTH, IMMUNE SUPPORT

1 large celery stalk
½ fennel bulb
1 cup strawberries
2 medium apples

Alternate ingredients, finishing with the apple.

Ingredient Tip: When juicing fennel, you can include the stems and leaves.

BOK JOY

MAKES ABOUT 12 OUNCES

BRAIN HEALTH, DETOXIFYING, HEART HEALTH, STRUCTURE SUPPORT

1 large bok choy stem
1 large orange, peeled
1 peach or nectarine,
  pit removed
1 cup raspberries
1 medium apple

Alternate ingredients, finishing with the apple.

SWISS ON THE BEACH

MAKES ABOUT 16 OUNCES

BRAIN HEALTH, ANTI-INFLAMMATORY, DIGESTION SUPPORT, MOOD LIFTER, STRUCTURE SUPPORT

1 cup pineapple
1 cup raspberries
2 large celery stalks
2 Swiss chard leaves
½ cucumber

Juice the pineapple and raspberries first if you want to reserve the pulp for another use. Alternate the remaining ingredients, finishing with the cucumber.

Pulp Tip: Add the pineapple and raspberry pulp to plain or low-sugar, plant-based yogurt for a healthy snack.

REAL HIGH C

MAKES ABOUT 16 OUNCES

BRAIN HEALTH, ANTI-INFLAMMATORY, HEART HEALTH, IMMUNE SUPPORT, MOOD LIFTER

1 medium lemon
1-inch piece fresh ginger
  root (optional)
1 orange bell pepper
4 small oranges, peeled

Alternate ingredients, finishing with the orange.

GARDEN GROVE

MAKES ABOUT 16 OUNCES

BRAIN HEALTH, HEART HEALTH, IMMUNE SUPPORT, MOOD LIFTER, STRUCTURE SUPPORT

1 orange, red, or yellow
  bell pepper

4 romaine leaves

2 small oranges, peeled

1 large cucumber

Alternate ingredients, finishing with the cucumber.

SWEET CITRUS TREAT

MAKES ABOUT 16 OUNCES

BRAIN HEALTH, ANTI-INFLAMMATORY, DIGESTION SUPPORT, MOOD LIFTER, STRUCTURE SUPPORT, WEIGHT LOSS

Handful spinach

1 large green apple

1 cup pineapple

12 parsley sprigs

1 pink or red
  grapefruit, peeled

Alternate ingredients, finishing with the grapefruit.

TROPICAL KALE DELIGHT

MAKES ABOUT 16 OUNCES

BRAIN HEALTH, ANTI-INFLAMMATORY, DETOXIFYING, HEART HEALTH, IMMUNE SUPPORT, MOOD LIFTER, WEIGHT LOSS

1 large celery stalk

2 kale leaves

½ pink or red
  grapefruit, peeled

1 Cara Cara or other small
  orange, peeled

½ cup pineapple

½ cucumber

Alternate ingredients, finishing with the cucumber.

BRAIN-BOOSTING GREENS WITH BLUEBERRIES

MAKES ABOUT 16 OUNCES

BRAIN HEALTH, HEART HEALTH, MOOD LIFTER, WEIGHT LOSS

1 kale leaf
4 romaine leaves
Handful spinach
1 green apple
1 cup blueberries
¼ lemon
1 medium cucumber

Alternate ingredients, finishing with the cucumber.

PINEAPPLE KICKS

MAKES ABOUT 16 OUNCES

BRAIN HEALTH, ANTI-INFLAMMATORY, DIGESTION SUPPORT, HEART HEALTH, STRUCTURE SUPPORT

1 yellow bell pepper
½ lemon
1-inch piece fresh
  ginger root
1-inch piece fresh
  turmeric root
2 cups pineapple
Freshly ground black
  pepper (optional)

Alternate the produce, finishing with the pineapple. Stir the black pepper (if using) directly into the juice to increase your absorption of the curcumin in the turmeric.

Ingredient Tip: If you don't have fresh turmeric, you can stir in ¼ teaspoon of ground turmeric at the end with the pepper. Make sure it is supplement grade or tested to be lead free.

SUNNY SWEET POTATO

MAKES ABOUT 16 OUNCES

BRAIN HEALTH, ANTI-INFLAMMATORY, HEART HEALTH, IMMUNE SUPPORT

2-inch piece broccoli stem

4 large celery stalks

1 small sweet potato, peeled

½ lemon

1-inch piece fresh turmeric root

3 small oranges, peeled

Freshly ground black pepper (optional)

Alternate the produce, finishing with the oranges. Stir the black pepper (if using) directly into the juice to increase your absorption of the curcumin in the turmeric.

TART ROOTS

MAKES ABOUT 16 OUNCES

BRAIN HEALTH, HEART HEALTH, STRUCTURE SUPPORT

1 medium golden or red beet

½ lemon

1 cup raspberries

2 large cucumbers

Alternate ingredients, finishing with the cucumber.

RASPBERRY AND KALE BRAIN BOOST

MAKES ABOUT 16 OUNCES

BRAIN HEALTH, DETOXIFYING, HEART HEALTH, MOOD LIFTER, STRUCTURE SUPPORT

4 kale leaves

½ lemon

1 cup raspberries

1 large cucumber

Alternate ingredients, finishing with the cucumber.

BERRYLICIOUS

MAKES ABOUT 16 OUNCES

BRAIN HEALTH, HEART HEALTH, STRUCTURE SUPPORT

½ large cucumber
2 kiwifruit
1 cup raspberries
4 teaspoons fresh mint
1 medium green apple

Alternate ingredients, finishing with the apple.

Substitution Tip: If you can't find kiwifruit, you can instead use a firm pear and half of a small lemon.

REFRESHING BLUEBERRY AND BASIL BLEND

MAKES ABOUT 16 OUNCES

BRAIN HEALTH, DIGESTION SUPPORT, HEART HEALTH, MOOD LIFTER, WEIGHT LOSS

Handful spinach
2 large Swiss chard leaves
1 cup blueberries
½ lemon
8 large basil leaves
2 large celery stalks

Alternate ingredients, finishing with the celery.

MY BERRY BEST

MAKES ABOUT 20 OUNCES

BRAIN HEALTH, DIGESTION SUPPORT, HEART HEALTH, STRUCTURE SUPPORT

1 cup blackberries
1 cup raspberries
2 kiwifruit
1 orange, peeled
2 large celery stalks
1 large cucumber

Juice the fruit first if you want to reserve the pulp for another use. Alternate the remaining ingredients, finishing with the cucumber.

ORANGE CHOY

MAKES ABOUT 20 OUNCES

BRAIN HEALTH, IMMUNE SUPPORT, STRUCTURE SUPPORT

2 large bok choy stems
½ lemon
1 orange, peeled
1 large cucumber

Alternate ingredients, finishing with the cucumber.

IN SHARP FOCUS

MAKES ABOUT 16 OUNCES

BRAIN HEALTH, DETOXIFYING, HEART HEALTH

4-inch piece
  broccoli stem
2 large carrots
1 cup blueberries
1 apple

Alternate ingredients, finishing with the apple.

POMEGRANATE-BLACKBERRY DELIGHT

MAKES ABOUT 16 OUNCES

BRAIN HEALTH, DIGESTION SUPPORT, HEART HEALTH

1 cup blackberries
½ lemon
½ cup pomegranate juice
4 large celery stalks

Alternate ingredients, finishing with the celery.

Ingredient Tip: One pomegranate contains about 1 cup of arils, which will yield ¼ to ½ cup of juice. If pomegranates are not in season, you can use freeze-dried pomegranate juice powder dissolved into cucumber juice, celery juice, or filtered water.

MINTED RASPBERRY COCKTAIL

MAKES ABOUT 16 OUNCES

BRAIN HEALTH, HEART HEALTH, STRUCTURE SUPPORT

1 apple
½ lemon
1 cup raspberries
4 teaspoons fresh mint
1 large cucumber

Alternate ingredients, ending with the cucumber.

BRAINY BLEND

MAKES ABOUT 24 OUNCES

BRAIN HEALTH, DIGESTION SUPPORT, HEART HEALTH, MOOD LIFTER, STRUCTURE SUPPORT, WEIGHT LOSS

2 large carrots
2 cups spinach
½ lemon
1 cup strawberries
1 apple

Alternate ingredients, finishing with the apple.

SUNNY SQUASH

MAKES ABOUT 16 OUNCES

BRAIN HEALTH, HEART HEALTH, IMMUNE SUPPORT, STRUCTURE SUPPORT

1 cup butternut squash
** or pumpkin**
4 Cara Cara oranges or
** 2 navel oranges, peeled**
1 large cucumber

Alternate ingredients, finishing with the cucumber.

SPRING GREENS

MAKES ABOUT 16 OUNCES

BRAIN HEALTH, DETOXIFYING, DIGESTION SUPPORT, MOOD LIFTER, STRUCTURE SUPPORT

1 cup cauliflower
Handful dandelion greens
2 kale leaves
1 orange, peeled
1 apple

Alternate ingredients, finishing with the apple.

SPICY BEET

MAKES ABOUT 10 OUNCES

BRAIN HEALTH, ANTI-INFLAMMATORY, DIGESTION SUPPORT, HEART HEALTH, MOOD LIFTER, STRUCTURE SUPPORT

1 medium golden or red beet
2 cups dandelion greens
½-inch piece fresh ginger root
½-inch piece fresh turmeric root
1 apple
Freshly ground black pepper (optional)

Alternate the produce, finishing with the apple. Stir the black pepper (if using) directly into the juice to increase your absorption of the curcumin in the turmeric.

CINNAMON APPLE PIE

MAKES ABOUT 16 OUNCES

BRAIN HEALTH, ANTI-INFLAMMATORY, DIGESTION SUPPORT, MOOD LIFTER

4 large celery stalks
1 small fennel bulb
1 apple
¼ teaspoon cinnamon

Alternate the produce, finishing with the apple. Stir the cinnamon directly into the juice or place the juice and the cinnamon in a jar and shake to combine.

SWEET POTATO PIE

MAKES ABOUT 16 OUNCES

BRAIN HEALTH, ANTI-INFLAMMATORY, STRUCTURE SUPPORT

2-inch piece fresh turmeric root

4 large carrots

1 small sweet potato, peeled

1 red apple

¼ teaspoon pumpkin pie spice

Freshly ground black pepper (optional)

Juice the turmeric root first, then alternate the remaining produce, finishing with the apple. Stir the pumpkin pie spice and the pepper directly into the juice or place the juice and the spices in a jar and shake to combine.

Substitution Tip: If you don't have pumpkin pie spice, you can use ¼ teaspoon of cinnamon instead.

BRAIN TEASER

MAKES ABOUT 24 OUNCES

BRAIN HEALTH, ANTI-INFLAMMATORY, HEART HEALTH, MOOD LIFTER, STRUCTURE SUPPORT, WEIGHT LOSS

2-inch piece fresh turmeric root

1 medium golden or red beet

Handful spinach

1 apple

½ lemon

1 large cucumber

Freshly ground black pepper (optional)

Juice the turmeric first, then alternate the remaining produce, finishing with the cucumber. Stir the black pepper (if using) directly into the juice to increase your absorption of the curcumin in the turmeric.

RASPBERRY SUNRISE

MAKES ABOUT 16 OUNCES

BRAIN HEALTH, HEART HEALTH, IMMUNE SUPPORT, MOOD LIFTER, STRUCTURE SUPPORT

1 medium golden beet
1 orange, peeled
1 cup raspberries
½ large cucumber

Alternate ingredients, finishing with the cucumber.

SWEET BELL KALE

MAKES ABOUT 16 OUNCES

BRAIN HEALTH, DETOXIFYING, HEART HEALTH, MOOD LIFTER, STRUCTURE SUPPORT

1 red bell pepper
4 kale leaves
1 small sweet potato, peeled
1 small lemon
1 large cucumber

Alternate ingredients, finishing with the cucumber.

FRESH SALSA

MAKES ABOUT 20 OUNCES

BRAIN HEALTH, DETOXIFYING, DIGESTION SUPPORT, HEART HEALTH, MOOD LIFTER, WEIGHT LOSS

1 to 2 teaspoons jalapeño pepper (optional)
1 red bell pepper
1 cup tomato
Handful cilantro
4 large celery stalks

Remove the seeds and membranes from the jalapeño pepper (if using) and juice it first. Alternate the remaining ingredients, finishing with the celery.

Substitution Tip: If you don't have a jalapeño pepper, try stirring in a pinch of cayenne pepper.

APPLE, KOHLRABI, AND KALE SIPPER

MAKES ABOUT 16 OUNCES

BRAIN HEALTH, DETOXIFYING, DIGESTION SUPPORT, MOOD LIFTER

2 large celery stalks
2 kale leaves
¼ small kohlrabi
½ lime, peeled
2 apples

Alternate ingredients, finishing with the apple.

GRAPEFRUIT AND KOHLRABI

MAKES ABOUT 16 OUNCES

BRAIN HEALTH, DETOXIFYING, DIGESTION SUPPORT, IMMUNE SUPPORT, WEIGHT LOSS

¼ small kohlrabi
½ pink or red grapefruit, peeled
2 large celery stalks
½ apple

Alternate ingredients, finishing with the apple or the celery.

SPRING HAS SPRUNG

MAKES ABOUT 16 OUNCES

BRAIN HEALTH, DETOXIFYING, HEART HEALTH

12 asparagus spears
4-inch piece broccoli stem
½ lemon
1 apple

Alternate ingredients, finishing with the apple.

CRUCIFEROUS GRAPEFRUIT BLEND

MAKES ABOUT 16 OUNCES

BRAIN HEALTH, DETOXIFYING, DIGESTION SUPPORT, IMMUNE SUPPORT, MOOD LIFTER, WEIGHT LOSS

2-inch piece broccoli stem

½ cup red cabbage

½ cup cauliflower

2 large carrots

½ pink or red grapefruit, peeled

Alternate ingredients, finishing with the grapefruit.

ORANGE RABBIT

MAKES ABOUT 20 OUNCES

BRAIN HEALTH, DETOXIFYING, IMMUNE SUPPORT, STRUCTURE SUPPORT

4-inch piece broccoli stem

4 large carrots

1 orange, peeled

4 large celery stalks

Alternate ingredients, finishing with the celery.

GOOD MORNING

MAKES ABOUT 16 OUNCES

BRAIN HEALTH, IMMUNE SUPPORT, MOOD LIFTER, STRUCTURE SUPPORT, WEIGHT LOSS

1 orange or red bell pepper

2 large carrots

1 pink or red grapefruit, peeled

Alternate ingredients, finishing with the grapefruit.

BERRY GOOD

MAKES ABOUT 16 OUNCES

BRAIN HEALTH, DETOXIFYING, HEART HEALTH, MOOD LIFTER

2 large bok choy stems
2 cups spinach
1 cup strawberries
Handful cilantro
½ lemon

Alternate ingredients, finishing with the lemon.

WALK IN THE PARK

MAKES ABOUT 20 OUNCES

BRAIN HEALTH, HEART HEALTH, MOOD LIFTER, STRUCTURE SUPPORT, WEIGHT LOSS

½ fennel bulb
2 large kale leaves
1 apple
1 large cucumber

Alternate ingredients, finishing with the cucumber.

SPICY SWEET POTATO

MAKES ABOUT 20 OUNCES

BRAIN HEALTH, ANTI-INFLAMMATORY, IMMUNE SUPPORT, MOOD LIFTER, WEIGHT LOSS

2-inch piece fresh
  ginger root
2-inch piece fresh
  turmeric root
1 small sweet
  potato, peeled
½ orange, red, or yellow
  bell pepper
2 cups spinach
1 large cucumber
Freshly ground black
  pepper (optional)

Alternate the ginger and the turmeric with the sweet potato, then alternate the remaining produce, finishing with the cucumber. Stir the black pepper (if using) directly into the juice to increase your absorption of the curcumin in the turmeric.

ORANGE POTATO BLISS

MAKES ABOUT 16 OUNCES

BRAIN HEALTH, ANTI-INFLAMMATORY, DIGESTION SUPPORT, IMMUNE SUPPORT

1- to 2-inch piece fresh
   turmeric root

1 large cucumber

1 small sweet
   potato, peeled

2 oranges, peeled

4 large celery stalks

Freshly ground black
   pepper (optional)

Juice the turmeric first, then alternate the remaining produce, finishing with the celery or the orange. Stir the black pepper (if using) directly into the juice to increase your absorption of the curcumin in the turmeric.

FINE AND DANDY

MAKES ABOUT 16 OUNCES

BRAIN HEALTH, ANTI-INFLAMMATORY, DETOXIFYING, HEART HEALTH, MOOD LIFTER, STRUCTURE SUPPORT

1-inch piece fresh
   turmeric root

2-inch piece
   broccoli stem

10 large dandelion leaves

½ fennel bulb

2 kale leaves

½ apple

1 orange, peeled

½ cucumber

Freshly ground black
   pepper (optional)

Juice the turmeric root first, then alternate the remaining produce, finishing with the cucumber. Stir the black pepper (if using) directly into the juice to increase your absorption of the curcumin in the turmeric.

SWEET SUMMER QUENCHER

MAKES ABOUT 20 OUNCES

BRAIN HEALTH, ANTI-INFLAMMATORY, HEART HEALTH, IMMUNE SUPPORT, MOOD LIFTER,
STRUCTURE SUPPORT

4 large romaine leaves
½ cucumber
1 orange, peeled
1 cup strawberries
1 small apple
1 cup watermelon

Alternate ingredients, finishing with the watermelon or the apple.

BRAINY COOLER

MAKES ABOUT 16 OUNCES

BRAIN HEALTH, ANTI-INFLAMMATORY, HEART HEALTH, STRUCTURE SUPPORT

1 cup blueberries
½ small lime, peeled
2 cups watermelon, with rind if organic
5 to 6 large green or purple basil leaves
½ medium cucumber

Alternate ingredients, finishing with the cucumber.

PLUM COCKTAIL

MAKES ABOUT 16 OUNCES

BRAIN HEALTH, DIGESTION SUPPORT, HEART HEALTH

1 cup black or red grapes
2 black or red plums, ripe but still firm
1-inch piece fresh ginger root
1 medium red apple

Alternate ingredients, finishing with the apple.

Pulp Tip: Freeze the pulp and use it later in a smoothie.

RUBY ROMANCE,
PAGE 49

HEAD START

MAKES ABOUT 16 OUNCES

BRAIN HEALTH, ANTI-INFLAMMATORY, DIGESTION SUPPORT, HEART HEALTH

1-inch piece fresh
  ginger root

2 large carrots

1 small zucchini

½ lemon

1 firm pear

1 medium apple

Juice the ginger root, then alternate the remaining ingredients, finishing with the apple.

Pulp Tip: Try using some of the pulp in place of shredded zucchini in a zucchini bread recipe.

RUBY ROMANCE

MAKES ABOUT 16 OUNCES

BRAIN HEALTH, DETOXIFYING, DIGESTION SUPPORT, HEART HEALTH, MOOD LIFTER

1 cup red cabbage

3 large celery stalks

2 cups black or red grapes

½ lemon

1 red apple

Alternate ingredients, finishing with the apple.

Add-in Tip: Add 2 teaspoons of apple cider vinegar for its weight-loss benefits and its balancing effect on blood sugar.

KEY LIME PIE

MAKES ABOUT 16 OUNCES

BRAIN HEALTH, DETOXIFYING, DIGESTION SUPPORT, HEART HEALTH, MOOD LIFTER, WEIGHT LOSS

3 large celery stalks

2 cups spinach

2 cups black or red grapes

3 key limes or
  ½ lime, peeled

2 small red apples

Alternate ingredients, finishing with the apple.

PURPLE PUNCH

MAKES ABOUT 16 OUNCES

BRAIN HEALTH, ANTI-INFLAMMATORY, DETOXIFYING, HEART HEALTH

2-inch piece
  broccoli stem
1 pound orange or
  purple carrots
1 cup blackberries
¼ lemon
1 orange, peeled
½-inch piece fresh
  ginger root
1 medium red apple

Alternate ingredients, finishing with the apple.

SUMMERTIME WATERMELON AND SWEET PEPPER SIPPER

MAKES ABOUT 16 OUNCES

BRAIN HEALTH, ANTI-INFLAMMATORY, HEART HEALTH, MOOD LIFTER

1 red bell pepper
3 teaspoons fresh mint
3 cups watermelon

Alternate ingredients, finishing with the watermelon.

SMOOTH OPERATOR

MAKES ABOUT 16 OUNCES

BRAIN HEALTH, ANTI-INFLAMMATORY, DIGESTION SUPPORT, MOOD LIFTER

1 mango
1 cup pineapple
1-inch piece fresh
  ginger root
1 pound carrots

Juice the mango and pineapple. Follow with the ginger and carrots.

Pulp Tip: Reserve the mango and pineapple pulp and add it to a smoothie or a fruit muffin recipe in place of the chopped fruit.

PURPLE PICK-ME-UP

MAKES ABOUT 16 OUNCES

BRAIN HEALTH, DETOXIFYING, HEART HEALTH, IMMUNE SUPPORT, MOOD LIFTER,
STRUCTURE SUPPORT

1 cup red cabbage

2 large carrots

½ apple

½ cup mango

1 cup strawberries

½ cucumber

Alternate ingredients, finishing with the cucumber.

COUNTRY STROLL

MAKES ABOUT 16 OUNCES

BRAIN HEALTH, DETOXIFYING, HEART HEALTH, MOOD LIFTER

1 cup blackberries

1 medium golden or
  red beet

1 orange, red, or yellow
  bell pepper

4 romaine leaves

2 bok choy stems

Juice the blackberries first, then alternate the
remaining ingredients, finishing with the bok choy.

STRAWBERRY, BASIL, AND BEET BLAST

MAKES ABOUT 16 OUNCES

BRAIN HEALTH, DETOXIFYING, HEART HEALTH, IMMUNE SUPPORT, MOOD LIFTER

1 medium golden or
  red beet

1 cup strawberries

6 large basil leaves

4 large celery stalks

Alternate ingredients, finishing with the celery.

SUNNY SPICE

MAKES ABOUT 16 OUNCES

BRAIN HEALTH, ANTI-INFLAMMATORY, HEART HEALTH, MOOD LIFTER, STRUCTURE SUPPORT

1 orange or red
   bell pepper

4 extra-large orange or
   purple carrots

1-inch piece fresh
   ginger root

½ large cucumber

Alternate ingredients, finishing with the cucumber.

FALL LEAVES

MAKES ABOUT 16 OUNCES

BRAIN HEALTH, ANTI-INFLAMMATORY, HEART HEALTH, MOOD LIFTER

2 small carrots

2 kale leaves

½ cup butternut squash
   or pumpkin

1-inch piece fresh
   turmeric root

2 small red apples

Pumpkin pie spice or
   cinnamon (optional)

Freshly ground black
   pepper (optional)

Alternate the produce, finishing with the apples. Stir the pumpkin pie spice and the pepper (if using) directly into the juice or place the juice and the spices in a jar and shake to combine.

ROYAL SIPPER

MAKES ABOUT 20 OUNCES

BRAIN HEALTH, DIGESTION SUPPORT, HEART HEALTH, IMMUNE SUPPORT, MOOD LIFTER

2 cups strawberries

2 cups red cabbage

1 red apple

Alternate ingredients, finishing with the apple.

Pulp Tip: Sprinkle some of the pulp on a salad to add some sweetness and raw cruciferous vegetables to your meal.

BERRY BERRY KALE

MAKES ABOUT 16 OUNCES

BRAIN HEALTH, DIGESTION SUPPORT, HEART HEALTH, IMMUNE SUPPORT, MOOD LIFTER

2 medium celery stalks
2 kale leaves
½ cup blackberries
½ cup strawberries
1 small lemon
1 large cucumber

Alternate ingredients, finishing with the cucumber.

MIDNIGHT BERRIES

MAKES ABOUT 16 OUNCES

BRAIN HEALTH, MOOD LIFTER, WEIGHT LOSS

½ cup blueberries
½ cup blackberries
2 large kale leaves
2 romaine leaves
1 large cucumber

Juice the berries first, then the kale and the romaine. Finish with the cucumber.

Pulp Tip: Reserve the berry pulp and spread it on toast.

POMEGRANATE AND KALE COCKTAIL

MAKES ABOUT 18 OUNCES

BRAIN HEALTH, ANTI-INFLAMMATORY, DETOXIFYING, HEART HEALTH, MOOD LIFTER

1 pomegranate
2 large kale leaves
¼ lemon
1 orange, peeled
**½-inch piece fresh
  ginger root**
1 red apple

Remove the arils from the pomegranate and run them through your juicer. Discard the peel. Alternate the remaining ingredients, finishing with the apple.

A.M. LEMON BOMB,
PAGE 77

CHAPTER 4

CLEANSING AND DETOXIFYING

What you eat and drink can enhance your body's efforts to cleanse and detoxify, ridding yourself of accumulated toxins, acids, and waste. Although all raw fruits and vegetables support detoxification and cleansing, raw fruit juice is especially astringent and high in antioxidants, so you'll see a lot of fruit juice blends in this chapter. You'll also see astringent bitter greens like dandelion, mustard greens, and collards.

Cruciferous vegetables like kale, radish, cauliflower, and broccoli contain glucosinolates that the body converts to anti-inflammatory isothiocyanates (ITCs) that enhance detoxification. These vegetables also provide your body with sulfur, which helps your liver produce glutathione, the master antioxidant. Beets and sweet potatoes are in this chapter for their beta-lains, which support detoxification. Parsley and spinach are rich in chlorophyll, which also supports the detoxification of carcinogens. Many of the recipes feature pears, plums, zucchini, and coconut water to help cleanse the bowels.

CLEANSING CARROT, BEET, AND CUCUMBER

MAKES ABOUT 16 OUNCES

CLEANSING, DETOXIFYING, ANTI-INFLAMMATORY, HEART HEALTH, MOOD LIFTER

1 medium golden or red beet

4 large carrots

1-inch piece fresh ginger root

1 small red apple

1 medium cucumber

Alternate ingredients, finishing with the cucumber.

Ingredient Tip: Peel the beet if you find the taste of beets too earthy for your palate.

SPICY CELERY

MAKES ABOUT 16 OUNCES

CLEANSING, DETOXIFYING, BRAIN HEALTH, DIGESTION SUPPORT, MOOD LIFTER

1 small mustard green leaf

1 large green apple

½ medium lemon

3 large celery stalks

Alternate ingredients, finishing with the celery.

GOOD GREENS

MAKES ABOUT 16 OUNCES

CLEANSING, DETOXIFYING, BONE HEALTH, MOOD LIFTER, WEIGHT LOSS

2 small mustard green leaves

2 large kale leaves

2 Swiss chard leaves

1 small lime, peeled

½ large cucumber

Alternate ingredients, finishing with the cucumber.

ORCHARD SALAD IN A GLASS

MAKES ABOUT 16 OUNCES

CLEANSING, DETOXIFYING, HEART HEALTH, IMMUNE SUPPORT, MOOD LIFTER, STRUCTURE SUPPORT

4 large romaine leaves
2 green apples
2 small oranges, peeled
8 parsley sprigs
1 large cucumber

Alternate ingredients, finishing with the cucumber.

DETOX SNACK

MAKES ABOUT 8 OUNCES

CLEANSING, DETOXIFYING, ANTI-INFLAMMATORY, DIGESTION SUPPORT, WEIGHT LOSS

Handful arugula
1-inch piece fresh ginger root
1 large celery stalk
1 medium green apple

Alternate ingredients, finishing with the apple or the celery.

GET YOUR GREENS

MAKES ABOUT 16 OUNCES

CLEANSING, DETOXIFYING, DIGESTION SUPPORT, MOOD LIFTER, STRUCTURE SUPPORT

Handful arugula
1 large celery stalk
Handful spinach
1 large cucumber

Alternate ingredients, finishing with the cucumber.

IT'S A BEAUTIFUL MORNING

MAKES ABOUT 16 OUNCES

CLEANSING, DETOXIFYING, ANTI-INFLAMMATORY, HEART HEALTH, IMMUNE SUPPORT, MOOD LIFTER

1 medium golden beet

1-inch piece fresh
   ginger root

1 large celery stalk

2 small oranges, peeled

Alternate ingredients, finishing with the orange or the celery.

SWEET SERENADE

MAKES ABOUT 16 OUNCES

CLEANSING, DETOXIFYING, DIGESTION SUPPORT, HEART HEALTH

1 medium apple

2 cups black, purple, or
   red grapes

2 firm pears

1 large celery stalk

Alternate ingredients, finishing with the celery.

DANDY PEAR

MAKES ABOUT 20 OUNCES

CLEANSING, DETOXIFYING, DIGESTION SUPPORT, STRUCTURE SUPPORT

2 medium bok
   choy stems

2 cups dandelion greens

1 firm pear

1 large cucumber

Alternate ingredients, finishing with the cucumber.

GRAPE AND FRIENDS

MAKES ABOUT 18 OUNCES

CLEANSING, DETOXIFYING, BRAIN HEALTH, DIGESTION SUPPORT, STRUCTURE SUPPORT

1 medium bok choy stem

1 large celery stalk

Handful dandelion greens

½ medium apple

1 cup black, purple, or red grapes

1 firm pear

½ large cucumber

Alternate ingredients, finishing with the cucumber.

Ingredient Tip: Juice the grape stems if they are fresh because they contain significant amounts of polyphenolic compounds, including a flavanonol called astilbin that is anti-inflammatory and a free-radical scavenger.

DELICIOUS DETOX

MAKES ABOUT 20 OUNCES

CLEANSING, DETOXIFYING, BRAIN HEALTH, DIGESTION SUPPORT, HEART HEALTH, MOOD LIFTER

1 cup red cabbage

2 cups black, purple, or red grapes

12 parsley sprigs

2 large celery stalks

Alternate ingredients, finishing with the celery.

QUICK AND EASY DETOX

MAKES ABOUT 16 OUNCES

CLEANSING, DETOXIFYING, DIGESTION SUPPORT, MOOD LIFTER

1 cup red cabbage

1 firm pear

8 medium romaine leaves

Alternate ingredients, finishing with the romaine.

DETOX DELIGHT

MAKES ABOUT 16 OUNCES

CLEANSING, DETOXIFYING, DIGESTION SUPPORT, MOOD LIFTER, STRUCTURE SUPPORT

1 medium zucchini
1 firm pear
Handful cilantro
½ large cucumber

Alternate ingredients, finishing with the cucumber.

CABBAGE, CUCUMBER, AND KALE COCKTAIL

MAKES ABOUT 16 OUNCES

CLEANSING, DETOXIFYING, BRAIN HEALTH, HEART HEALTH, MOOD LIFTER, STRUCTURE SUPPORT

1 cup red cabbage
2 medium kale leaves
1 medium red apple
½ red or black plum
½ large cucumber

Alternate ingredients, finishing with the cucumber.

BASIC BOK CHOY BLEND

MAKES ABOUT 20 OUNCES

CLEANSING, DETOXIFYING, BRAIN HEALTH, HEART HEALTH

1 medium zucchini
2 cups black, purple, or red grapes
4 small bok choy stems

Alternate ingredients, finishing with the bok choy.

CLEANSING CARROT

MAKES ABOUT 16 OUNCES

CLEANSING, DETOXIFYING, HEART HEALTH, IMMUNE SUPPORT, MOOD LIFTER

4 large carrots
Handful parsley
1 firm pear

Alternate ingredients, finishing with the pear.

YUMMY PLUM

MAKES ABOUT 16 OUNCES

CLEANSING, DETOXIFYING, DIGESTION SUPPORT, HEART HEALTH, MOOD LIFTER

4 medium kale leaves

**1 cup black, purple, or
red grapes**

1 black or red plum

2 large celery stalks

Alternate ingredients, finishing with the celery.

FRESH DETOX

MAKES ABOUT 16 OUNCES

CLEANSING, DETOXIFYING, HEART HEALTH, IMMUNE SUPPORT, MOOD LIFTER

4 large dandelion leaves

2 medium radishes

1 medium zucchini

Handful cilantro

**1 cup black, purple, or
red grapes**

**1 small orange, red, or
yellow bell pepper**

Alternate ingredients, finishing with the bell pepper.

CARROT-APPLE DETOX

MAKES ABOUT 20 OUNCES

CLEANSING, DETOXIFYING, DIGESTION SUPPORT, HEART HEALTH, IMMUNE SUPPORT, MOOD LIFTER, STRUCTURE SUPPORT

4 medium carrots
12 parsley sprigs
1 medium apple
2 medium celery stalks
1 large cucumber

Alternate ingredients, finishing with the cucumber.

CLEANSING CARROT AND TURMERIC COCKTAIL

MAKES ABOUT 16 OUNCES

CLEANSING, DETOXIFYING, ANTI-INFLAMMATORY, HEART HEALTH, IMMUNE SUPPORT, MOOD LIFTER

4 medium carrots
1-inch piece fresh turmeric root
Handful parsley
1 large orange, red, or yellow bell pepper
Freshly ground black pepper (optional)

Alternate the produce, finishing with the bell pepper. Stir the black pepper (if using) directly into the juice to increase your absorption of the curcumin in the turmeric.

CARROT AND SPINACH DETOX

MAKES ABOUT 16 OUNCES

CLEANSING, DETOXIFYING, ANTI-INFLAMMATORY, BRAIN HEALTH, HEART HEALTH, MOOD LIFTER, WEIGHT LOSS

1 large orange, red, or
   yellow bell pepper

2 large carrots

Handful spinach

1 small lemon

1-inch piece fresh
   turmeric root

Handful cilantro

½ large cucumber

Freshly ground black
   pepper (optional)

Alternate the produce, finishing with the cucumber. Stir the black pepper (if using) directly into the juice to increase your absorption of the curcumin in the turmeric.

STRAWBERRY TART

MAKES ABOUT 16 OUNCES

CLEANSING, DETOXIFYING, BRAIN HEALTH, DIGESTION SUPPORT, IMMUNE SUPPORT MOOD LIFTER

1 cup strawberries

1 cup cauliflower

4 medium romaine leaves

4 medium celery stalks

Alternate ingredients, finishing with the celery.

STRAWBERRY SPRINGS

MAKES ABOUT 16 OUNCES

CLEANSING, DETOXIFYING, BRAIN HEALTH, HEART HEALTH, IMMUNE SUPPORT

1 cup strawberries

1 cup black, purple, or red grapes

4 medium radishes

1 large orange, red, or yellow bell pepper

Alternate ingredients, finishing with the bell pepper.

CAULIFLOWER CLEANSE

MAKES ABOUT 16 OUNCES

CLEANSING, DETOXIFYING, BRAIN HEALTH, DIGESTION SUPPORT, MOOD LIFTER

1 cup cauliflower

1 firm pear

8 parsley sprigs

4 large celery stalks

Alternate ingredients, finishing with the celery.

YUMMY BERRY CLEANSER

MAKES ABOUT 16 OUNCES

CLEANSING, DETOXIFYING, BRAIN HEALTH, DIGESTION SUPPORT, HEART HEALTH, MOOD LIFTER

1 cup mixed berries

1 firm pear

4 cups spinach

4 medium celery stalks

Juice the berries and the pear first, then alternate the remaining ingredients, finishing with the celery.

Pulp Tip: Reserve the berry and pear pulp as a spread for bread or toast.

BEST FRIENDS

MAKES ABOUT 16 OUNCES

CLEANSING, DETOXIFYING, ANTI-INFLAMMATORY, BRAIN HEALTH, STRUCTURE SUPPORT

4 kale leaves
2 cups pineapple

Alternate ingredients, finishing with the pineapple.

Pulp Tip: Reserve the pulp for a smoothie.

FRESH CLEANSE

MAKES ABOUT 16 OUNCES

CLEANSING, DETOXIFYING, IMMUNE SUPPORT

1 red bell pepper
2 large carrots
1 small collard leaf
1 medium kale leaf
½ large cucumber
**Handful cilantro
  or parsley**
1 medium red apple

Alternate ingredients, finishing with the apple.

Equipment Tip: If you are using a centrifugal juicer, roll up or ball up your leafy greens and juice them between the carrots for an increased yield.

PURPLE PINEAPPLE

MAKES ABOUT 16 OUNCES

CLEANSING, DETOXIFYING, BRAIN HEALTH, DIGESTION SUPPORT, IMMUNE SUPPORT, MOOD LIFTER, STRUCTURE SUPPORT

1 cup red cabbage
Handful spinach
1 cup pineapple
**2 Cara Cara or other
  small oranges, peeled**

Alternate ingredients, finishing with the orange or the pineapple.

BIG COCONUT CLEANSE

MAKES ABOUT 28 OUNCES

CLEANSING, DETOXIFYING, BRAIN HEALTH, DIGESTION SUPPORT, MOOD LIFTER

4-inch piece broccoli stem

4 large kale leaves

2 medium radishes

1 medium zucchini

1 firm pear

1 medium apple

1 cup fresh coconut water

Alternate the produce, finishing with the apple. Stir the coconut water directly into the juice.

CLEAN AND GREEN

MAKES ABOUT 20 OUNCES

CLEANSING, DETOXIFYING, DIGESTION SUPPORT, HEART HEALTH, MOOD LIFTER, STRUCTURE SUPPORT

4-inch piece broccoli stem

4 large Swiss chard leaves

1 medium apple

2 large celery stalks

Alternate ingredients, finishing with the celery or the apple.

GRAPE-CABBAGE CURE

MAKES ABOUT 16 OUNCES

CLEANSING, DETOXIFYING, BRAIN HEALTH, HEART HEALTH, MOOD LIFTER, STRUCTURE SUPPORT

1 cup red cabbage

2 cups black, purple, or red grapes

12 parsley sprigs

1 medium apple

Alternate ingredients, finishing with the apple.

HEAVENLY KALE

MAKES ABOUT 20 OUNCES

CLEANSING, DETOXIFYING, ANTI-INFLAMMATORY, DIGESTION SUPPORT, HEART HEALTH,
STRUCTURE SUPPORT

2 large kale leaves
1 cup pineapple
2 cups watermelon

Alternate ingredients, finishing with the watermelon or the pineapple.

SUMMER CARROT SIPPER

MAKES ABOUT 16 OUNCES

CLEANSING, DETOXIFYING, ANTI-INFLAMMATORY, HEART HEALTH, MOOD LIFTER, STRUCTURE
SUPPORT

2 large carrots
2 large kale leaves
½ red apple
1 cup watermelon

Alternate ingredients, finishing with the watermelon.

KIWI-MELON REFRESHER

MAKES ABOUT 16 OUNCES

CLEANSING, DETOXIFYING, ANTI-INFLAMMATORY, HEART HEALTH, IMMUNE SUPPORT

2 large bok choy stems
2 kiwifruit
1 cup watermelon

Alternate ingredients, finishing with the watermelon.

CALL ME SWEETHEART

MAKES ABOUT 16 OUNCES

CLEANSING, DETOXIFYING, ANTI-INFLAMMATORY, DIGESTION SUPPORT, HEART HEALTH,
IMMUNE SUPPORT, MOOD LIFTER, STRUCTURE SUPPORT

Handful spinach

2 kiwifruit

1 small lime, peeled

1 cup pineapple

1 cup watermelon

4 small celery stalks

Alternate ingredients, finishing with the celery or the watermelon.

SWISS LEMON

MAKES ABOUT 16 OUNCES

CLEANSING, DETOXIFYING, MOOD LIFTER, STRUCTURE SUPPORT

4 medium Swiss
  chard leaves

1 lemon

2 large bok choy stems

Alternate ingredients, finishing with the bok choy.

GREEN PEAR

MAKES ABOUT 16 OUNCES

CLEANSING, DETOXIFYING, DIGESTION SUPPORT, MOOD LIFTER, WEIGHT LOSS

4 cups spinach

½ lemon

2 firm pears

Alternate ingredients, finishing with the pear.

BLUEBERRIES ON THE BEACH

MAKES ABOUT 20 OUNCES

CLEANSING, DETOXIFYING, BRAIN HEALTH, DIGESTION SUPPORT, MOOD LIFTER

4 cups spinach
1 medium zucchini
½ cup blueberries
½ small lemon
1 cup pineapple
½ cup fresh
   coconut water

Alternate the produce, finishing with the pineapple. Stir the coconut water directly into the juice.

ORCHARD COLLARDS

MAKES ABOUT 16 OUNCES

CLEANSING, DETOXIFYING, HEART HEALTH, MOOD LIFTER

4 small collard leaves
1 firm pear
2 medium apples

Alternate ingredients, finishing with the apple.

BOK CHOY BERRY

MAKES ABOUT 20 OUNCES

CLEANSING, DETOXIFYING, BRAIN HEALTH

4 small bok choy stems
1 medium zucchini
1 cup blackberries
½ cup fresh
   coconut water

Alternate the bok choy, zucchini, and blackberries. Stir the coconut water directly into the juice.

PURPLE PEAR

MAKES ABOUT 16 OUNCES

CLEANSING, DETOXIFYING, BRAIN HEALTH, DIGESTION SUPPORT

12 dandelion leaves
1 cup blueberries
½ medium lemon
1 firm pear
4 large celery stalks

Alternate ingredients, finishing with the celery.

DANDELION BELL

MAKES ABOUT 16 OUNCES

CLEANSING, DETOXIFYING, BRAIN HEALTH, HEART HEALTH, IMMUNE SUPPORT, MOOD LIFTER

4 dandelion leaves
½ medium lemon
2 small apples
1 orange, red, or yellow
  bell pepper

Alternate ingredients, finishing with the bell pepper or the apple.

GREENS AND GARDEN

MAKES ABOUT 16 OUNCES

CLEANSING, DETOXIFYING, BRAIN HEALTH, HEART HEALTH, IMMUNE SUPPORT, MOOD LIFTER

4 small carrots
2 large kale leaves
1 medium zucchini
8 parsley sprigs
1 orange, red, or yellow
  bell pepper

Alternate ingredients, finishing with the bell pepper.

HEARTY CARROT-KALE DETOX

MAKES ABOUT 24 OUNCES

CLEANSING, DETOXIFYING, HEART HEALTH

4 extra-large carrots
2 large kale leaves
**1 small sweet
   potato, peeled**

Alternate ingredients, finishing with the sweet potato.

Pulp Tip: Carrot-veggie pulp like this can be made into fritters. Season with salt (or no-salt seasoning), pepper, and chili powder. Form into patties and bake at 350°F for 10 to 15 minutes, then flip and bake for 10 to 15 minutes more, or until golden. (If your pulp is very dry, you can add a "flax egg." Mix 1 tablespoon of ground flaxseed with 2½ tablespoons of warm water and allow it to sit until it thickens.) Enjoy these patties in a pita with plain soy yogurt or add them to a salad.

VEGGIE CLEANSER

MAKES ABOUT 16 OUNCES

CLEANSING, DETOXIFYING, BRAIN HEALTH, DIGESTION SUPPORT, HEART HEALTH, MOOD LIFTER, WEIGHT LOSS

3 cups spinach
**½ small sweet
   potato, peeled**
8 parsley sprigs
½ medium lemon
4 large celery stalks

Alternate ingredients, finishing with the celery.

SWEET POTATO AND PEPPER PUNCH

MAKES ABOUT 16 OUNCES

CLEANSING, DETOXIFYING, BRAIN HEALTH, HEART HEALTH, IMMUNE SUPPORT, MOOD LIFTER, STRUCTURE SUPPORT

1 orange, red, or yellow
  bell pepper

1 small sweet
  potato, peeled

Handful parsley

1 large cucumber

Alternate ingredients, finishing with the cucumber.

SWEET POTATO GREENS

MAKES ABOUT 16 OUNCES

CLEANSING, DETOXIFYING, BONE HEALTH, BRAIN HEALTH, MOOD LIFTER, STRUCTURE SUPPORT

6 small dandelion leaves

2 large kale leaves

½ small sweet
  potato, peeled

2 large Swiss chard leaves

1 medium apple

½ large cucumber

Alternate ingredients, finishing with the cucumber.

GRAPE LEMONADE

MAKES ABOUT 16 OUNCES

CLEANSING, DETOXIFYING, BRAIN HEALTH, HEART HEALTH

2 cups black, purple, or
  red grapes

½ medium lemon

2 medium apples

Alternate ingredients, finishing with the apple.

ORANGE ROOTS

MAKES ABOUT 16 OUNCES

CLEANSING, DETOXIFYING, ANTI-INFLAMMATORY, BRAIN HEALTH, HEART HEALTH

4 large carrots

1-inch piece fresh turmeric root

1 small sweet potato, peeled

Freshly ground black pepper (optional)

Alternate the produce, finishing with the sweet potato. Stir the black pepper (if using) directly into the juice to increase your absorption of the curcumin in the turmeric.

Add-in Tip: Add ¼ teaspoon of ground cinnamon directly into the juice for a brain boost.

BEETROOT DETOX

MAKES ABOUT 16 OUNCES

CLEANSING, DETOXIFYING, ANTI-INFLAMMATORY, HEART HEALTH, MOOD LIFTER, STRUCTURE SUPPORT

1 medium golden or red beet

1-inch piece fresh ginger root

1-inch piece fresh turmeric root

12 parsley sprigs

1 medium red apple

1 large cucumber

Freshly ground black pepper (optional)

Alternate the produce, finishing with the cucumber. Stir the black pepper (if using) directly into the juice to increase your absorption of the curcumin in the turmeric.

BRIGHT MORNING

MAKES ABOUT 16 OUNCES

CLEANSING, DETOXIFYING, BRAIN HEALTH, DIGESTION SUPPORT, HEART HEALTH, IMMUNE SUPPORT, MOOD LIFTER, STRUCTURE SUPPORT

3 large carrots

2 large celery stalks

Handful spinach

8 parsley sprigs

2 medium oranges, peeled

½ large cucumber

Alternate ingredients, finishing with the cucumber.

GARNET DETOX

MAKES ABOUT 16 OUNCES

CLEANSING, DETOXIFYING, HEART HEALTH, MOOD LIFTER, STRUCTURE SUPPORT

½ medium red beet

2 beet stems with greens, or handful spinach

4 parsley sprigs

3 large carrots

1 small lemon

1 medium red apple

Alternate ingredients, finishing with the apple.

CHLOROPHYLL CLEANSE

MAKES ABOUT 16 OUNCES

CLEANSING, DETOXIFYING, MOOD LIFTER, STRUCTURE SUPPORT, WEIGHT LOSS

2 large celery stalks

1 large kale leaf

2 cups spinach

1 large Swiss chard leaf

2 green apples

**8 parsley or
cilantro sprigs**

1 large cucumber

Alternate ingredients, finishing with the cucumber.

Add-in Tip: For enhanced detoxification support, add a serving of chlorella powder. This green algae may enhance your body's ability to remove heavy metals like lead, cadmium, and mercury.

LEMON-LIME DETOX

MAKES ABOUT 16 OUNCES

CLEANSING, DETOXIFYING, ANTI-INFLAMMATORY, DIGESTION SUPPORT, HEART HEALTH, MOOD LIFTER

¼ medium lemon

¼ medium lime, peeled

**1-inch piece fresh
ginger root**

Handful cilantro

1 pound carrots

**½ cup fresh
coconut water**

Alternate the produce. Stir the coconut water directly into the juice.

CAULIFLOWER GREENS

MAKES ABOUT 16 OUNCES

CLEANSING, DETOXIFYING, BRAIN HEALTH, IMMUNE SUPPORT, MOOD LIFTER, STRUCTURE SUPPORT, WEIGHT LOSS

1 cup cauliflower
3 large kale leaves
Handful spinach
1 orange, peeled
1 apple

Alternate ingredients, finishing with the apple.

SPICED GREEN APPLE

MAKES ABOUT 16 OUNCES

CLEANSING, DETOXIFYING, BRAIN HEALTH, DIGESTION SUPPORT, HEART HEALTH, MOOD LIFTER, WEIGHT LOSS

1 small mustard green leaf
Handful spinach
1 large celery stalk
2 green apples
1 teaspoon ground cinnamon (optional)

Alternate the produce, finishing with the apple. Stir the cinnamon (if using) directly into the juice or place the juice and the cinnamon in a jar and shake to combine.

ZUCCHINI, GRAPE, AND CELERY BLEND

MAKES ABOUT 16 OUNCES

CLEANSING, DETOXIFYING, BRAIN HEALTH, DIGESTION SUPPORT

2 cups black, purple, or red grapes
1 medium zucchini
4 large celery stalks

Alternate ingredients, finishing with the celery.

A.M. LEMON BOMB

MAKES ABOUT 4 OUNCES

CLEANSING, DETOXIFYING, ANTI-INFLAMMATORY, DIGESTION SUPPORT

¼ medium lemon

¼-inch piece fresh
  ginger root

¼-inch piece fresh
  turmeric root

1 large celery stalk

½ green apple

Freshly ground black
  pepper (optional)

Alternate the produce, finishing with the apple. Stir the black pepper (if using) directly into the juice to increase your absorption of the curcumin in the turmeric.

Equipment Tip: If you have a slow or single-auger juicer, double this recipe and reserve a serving for the next day. It's a delicious, cleansing way to start the day!

SWEET-TART

MAKES ABOUT 16 OUNCES

CLEANSING, DETOXIFYING, ANTI-INFLAMMATORY, IMMUNE SUPPORT

1 medium golden or
  red beet

1 large Swiss chard leaf

2 Cara Cara or other
  small oranges, peeled

5 parsley sprigs

3 large celery stalks

Alternate ingredients, finishing with the celery.

TROPICAL BOK CHOY

MAKES ABOUT 16 OUNCES

CLEANSING, DETOXIFYING, ANTI-INFLAMMATORY, DIGESTION SUPPORT

4 medium bok
  choy stems

1 cup pineapple

1 cup fresh coconut water

Alternate the bok choy and the pineapple. Stir the coconut water directly into the juice.

PEPPER, CARROT,
AND APPLE BLEND,
PAGE 89

CHAPTER 5

DIGESTION

The juice ingredients and blends in this chapter support various parts of the digestive tract, from the esophagus to the bowels. Ginger is well-known for relieving nausea and vomiting. Pears contain phytonutrients that can reduce the risk of gastric and esophageal cancers. The digestive enzymes in pineapple and papaya help improve the digestion of proteins. Parsley and fennel juice can help relieve bloating and cramping.

If you suffer from indigestion or acid reflux, fresh coconut water may give you some relief. Celery juice contains antioxidants and anti-inflammatory nutrients that support the entire digestive tract, and it may decrease the risk of gastric ulcers. Cabbage juice can help prevent and heal peptic ulcers.

If you suffer from constipation, apples, pears, grapes, and stone fruits may help because they contain sorbitol, which pulls water into the large intestine to make stools easier to pass. Foods high in vitamin C like lemons, kiwifruit, mango, pineapple, papaya, and fennel also help pull water into the bowels. Spinach juice encourages peristalsis for regular bowel movements. Blackberries are highly anti-inflammatory and have positive effects for people with inflammatory bowel disease.

HINT OF SPRING

MAKES ABOUT 12 OUNCES

DIGESTION SUPPORT, DETOXIFYING, STRUCTURE SUPPORT, WEIGHT LOSS

**8 medium
  asparagus spears**
2 large celery stalks
5 parsley sprigs
1 medium apple

Alternate ingredients, finishing with the apple.

4C JUICE

MAKES ABOUT 16 OUNCES

DIGESTION SUPPORT, BRAIN HEALTH, DETOXIFYING, HEART HEALTH, STRUCTURE SUPPORT

2 cups red cabbage
2 medium carrots
1 small collard leaf
1 small apple
½ cucumber

Alternate ingredients, finishing with the cucumber.

CELERY, SPINACH, AND KIWI BLEND

MAKES ABOUT 16 OUNCES

DIGESTION SUPPORT, HEART HEALTH, STRUCTURE SUPPORT, WEIGHT LOSS

5 large celery stalks
3 cups spinach
2 kiwifruit
1 large cucumber

Alternate ingredients, finishing with the cucumber.

QUICK DIGESTIVE SUPPORT

MAKES ABOUT 16 OUNCES

DIGESTION SUPPORT, HEART HEALTH, IMMUNE SUPPORT

4 large celery stalks
2 kiwifruit
2 medium green apples

Alternate ingredients, finishing with the apple.

SMOOTH MOVE

MAKES ABOUT 18 OUNCES

DIGESTION SUPPORT, STRUCTURE SUPPORT, WEIGHT LOSS

Handful spinach
½ large lemon
2 pears
4 large celery stalks

Alternate ingredients, finishing with the celery.

GINGERED PINEAPPLE

MAKES ABOUT 16 OUNCES

DIGESTION SUPPORT, ANTI-INFLAMMATORY, HEART HEALTH, STRUCTURE SUPPORT

**1-inch piece fresh
   ginger root**
1 cup pineapple
**½ cup fresh
   coconut water**

Juice the ginger and follow with the pineapple. Stir the coconut water directly into the juice.

TROPICAL DIGESTIVE

MAKES ABOUT 16 OUNCES

DIGESTION SUPPORT, ANTI-INFLAMMATORY, DETOXIFYING, HEART HEALTH, STRUCTURE SUPPORT

1 cup pineapple

6 parsley sprigs

½ large lemon

4 small celery stalks

1 cup fresh coconut water

Alternate the produce, finishing with the celery. Stir the coconut water directly into the juice.

MANGO MEMORIES

MAKES ABOUT 16 OUNCES

DIGESTION SUPPORT, ANTI-INFLAMMATORY, DETOXIFYING, HEART HEALTH, IMMUNE SUPPORT, STRUCTURE SUPPORT

1 cup mango

Handful parsley

1 cup pineapple

4 small celery stalks

1 cup fresh coconut water

Alternate the produce, finishing with the celery. Stir the coconut water directly into the juice.

MINTED MANGO

MAKES ABOUT 16 OUNCES

DIGESTION SUPPORT, ANTI-INFLAMMATORY, IMMUNE SUPPORT, STRUCTURE SUPPORT

1 cup mango

1 cup pineapple

½ large lemon

24 small fresh
   mint leaves

4 large celery stalks

Alternate ingredients, finishing with the celery.

CELERY IN PARADISE

MAKES ABOUT 28 OUNCES

DIGESTION SUPPORT, ANTI-INFLAMMATORY, IMMUNE SUPPORT, STRUCTURE SUPPORT

1 cup pineapple
1 cup mango
Handful spinach
½ large lemon
4 large celery stalks

Alternate ingredients, finishing with the celery.

GRAPE, APPLE, AND MANGO TONIC

MAKES ABOUT 16 OUNCES

DIGESTION SUPPORT, DETOXIFYING, HEART HEALTH, IMMUNE SUPPORT

1 cup black, purple, or red grapes
½ large lemon
1 cup mango
2 small apples

Alternate ingredients, finishing with the apple.

PLUM, MANGO, AND APPLE CURE

MAKES ABOUT 16 OUNCES

DIGESTION SUPPORT, BRAIN HEALTH, HEART HEALTH, IMMUNE SUPPORT

1 cup mango
2 black or red plums
2 small apples

Alternate ingredients, finishing with the apple.

PLUM AND MANGO COCKTAIL

MAKES ABOUT 20 OUNCES

DIGESTION SUPPORT, ANTI-INFLAMMATORY, BRAIN HEALTH, IMMUNE SUPPORT

2 cups mango
Handful spinach
1 large lemon
1-inch piece fresh ginger root
2 black or red plums
1 large cucumber

Juice the mango first, then alternate the remaining ingredients, finishing with the cucumber.

Pulp Tip: Depending on your juicer, there may be a good amount of mango pulp that you can freeze and add to a smoothie.

PINEAPPLE AND BOK CHOY

MAKES ABOUT 16 OUNCES

DIGESTION SUPPORT, ANTI-INFLAMMATORY, BRAIN HEALTH, DETOXIFYING, STRUCTURE SUPPORT

4 large bok choy stems
1 cup pineapple
9 cilantro sprigs
1 lime, peeled
1½ cucumbers

Alternate ingredients, finishing with the cucumber.

GARDEN MANGO

MAKES ABOUT 16 OUNCES

DIGESTION SUPPORT, STRUCTURE SUPPORT

1 cup mango
Handful parsley
1 medium zucchini
½ large lemon
4 large celery stalks

Alternate ingredients, finishing with the celery.

SWISS GRAPES

MAKES ABOUT 24 OUNCES

DIGESTION SUPPORT, BRAIN HEALTH, DETOXIFYING, HEART HEALTH

2 large Swiss chard leaves
1 medium zucchini
½ large lemon
1 cup black, purple, or
   red grapes
2 small apples

Alternate ingredients, finishing with the apple.

FENNEL AND CELERY DIGESTIVE

MAKES ABOUT 16 OUNCES

DIGESTION SUPPORT, STRUCTURE SUPPORT, WEIGHT LOSS

1 small fennel bulb
Handful spinach
½ large lemon
4 large celery stalks

Alternate ingredients, finishing with the celery.

CABBAGE, GRAPE, AND PEAR BLEND

MAKES ABOUT 20 OUNCES

DIGESTION SUPPORT, BRAIN HEALTH, DETOXIFYING, HEART HEALTH

1 cup red cabbage
1 cup black, purple, or
   red grapes
12 parsley sprigs
1 firm pear
4 large celery stalks

Alternate ingredients, finishing with the celery.

SWISS PEAR

MAKES ABOUT 20 OUNCES

DIGESTION SUPPORT, BRAIN HEALTH, DETOXIFYING, STRUCTURE SUPPORT

2 large Swiss chard leaves
½ large lemon
Handful parsley
1 firm pear
4 large celery stalks

Alternate ingredients, finishing with the celery.

FENNEL AND APPLE DIGESTIVE

MAKES ABOUT 16 OUNCES

DIGESTION SUPPORT, DETOXIFYING, STRUCTURE SUPPORT

1 small fennel bulb
12 large basil leaves
12 parsley sprigs
4 medium celery stalks
1 small apple

Alternate ingredients, finishing with the apple.

SIMPLE CABBAGE AND FENNEL BLEND

MAKES ABOUT 16 OUNCES

DIGESTION SUPPORT, BRAIN HEALTH, HEART HEALTH, WEIGHT LOSS

2 cups red cabbage
2 small fennel bulbs

Alternate ingredients, finishing with the fennel.

GO PURPLE

MAKES ABOUT 20 OUNCES

DIGESTION SUPPORT, BRAIN HEALTH, HEART HEALTH, STRUCTURE SUPPORT

1 cup red cabbage
2 large celery stalks
1 small fennel bulb
½ large lemon
1 small red apple

Alternate ingredients, finishing with the apple.

GET REGULAR

MAKES ABOUT 16 OUNCES

DIGESTION SUPPORT, BRAIN HEALTH, HEART HEALTH

4 cups spinach
½ large lemon
4 large carrots

Alternate ingredients, finishing with the carrot.

SWEET AND SALTY

MAKES ABOUT 16 OUNCES

DIGESTION SUPPORT, BRAIN HEALTH, DETOXIFYING

8 medium Swiss chard leaves
Handful parsley
2 cups black, purple, or red grapes

Alternate ingredients, finishing with the grapes.

MINTED CABBAGE KALE

MAKES ABOUT 16 OUNCES

DIGESTION SUPPORT, BRAIN HEALTH, HEART HEALTH, WEIGHT LOSS

8 medium kale leaves
½ large lemon
½ cup fresh mint
1 cup red cabbage

Alternate ingredients, finishing with the cabbage.

GAS RELIEVER

MAKES ABOUT 24 OUNCES

DIGESTION SUPPORT, DETOXIFYING, HEART HEALTH, STRUCTURE SUPPORT

1 green bell pepper
12 parsley sprigs
½ large lemon
8 large carrots

Alternate ingredients, finishing with the carrot.

GREEN REFRESHER

MAKES ABOUT 16 OUNCES

DIGESTION SUPPORT, STRUCTURE SUPPORT, WEIGHT LOSS

1 green bell pepper
2 medium celery stalks
1 medium zucchini
1 green apple

Alternate ingredients, finishing with the apple.

ZUCCHINI, CARROT, AND APPLE BLEND

MAKES ABOUT 20 OUNCES

DIGESTION SUPPORT, DETOXIFYING, HEART HEALTH

4 medium carrots
12 parsley sprigs
1 medium zucchini
1 medium apple

Alternate ingredients, finishing with the apple.

TART APPLE SALAD

MAKES ABOUT 16 OUNCES

DIGESTION SUPPORT, BRAIN HEALTH, DETOXIFYING, HEART HEALTH, MOOD LIFTER

4 small kale leaves
4 large romaine leaves
Handful spinach
2 green apples

Alternate ingredients, finishing with the apple.

BLACKBERRY HYDRATOR

MAKES ABOUT 16 OUNCES

DIGESTION SUPPORT, BRAIN HEALTH, CLEANSING, HEART HEALTH, STRUCTURE SUPPORT

2 cups blackberries
2 firm pears
8 medium celery stalks

Alternate ingredients, finishing with the celery.

PEPPER, CARROT, AND APPLE BLEND

MAKES ABOUT 16 OUNCES

DIGESTION SUPPORT, HEART HEALTH, STRUCTURE SUPPORT

1 green bell pepper
4 large carrots
1 small apple

Alternate ingredients, finishing with the apple.

SUMMER BLACKBERRY

MAKES ABOUT 16 OUNCES

DIGESTION SUPPORT, BRAIN HEALTH, DETOXIFYING, HEART HEALTH, MOOD LIFTER, STRUCTURE SUPPORT

4 medium kale leaves
4 small celery stalks
1 cup blackberries
12 parsley sprigs
2 large romaine leaves
1 small apple

Alternate ingredients, finishing with the apple.

PLUM GOOD

MAKES ABOUT 16 OUNCES

DIGESTION SUPPORT, BRAIN HEALTH, CLEANSING, HEART HEALTH, STRUCTURE SUPPORT

1 cup blackberries
2 black or red plums
8 small celery stalks

Alternate ingredients, finishing with the celery.

SWISS PLUM

MAKES ABOUT 20 OUNCES

DIGESTION SUPPORT, BRAIN HEALTH, CLEANSING, DETOXIFYING, HEART HEALTH, MOOD LIFTER, STRUCTURE SUPPORT

2 large celery stalks
4 medium Swiss
  chard leaves
2 black or red plums
Handful parsley
½ cucumber

Alternate ingredients, finishing with the cucumber.

CARA CARA CARROT

DIGESTION SUPPORT, DETOXIFYING, HEART HEALTH, IMMUNE SUPPORT, STRUCTURE SUPPORT

2 large carrots
8 parsley sprigs
2 Cara Cara or other
  small oranges, peeled
1 small red apple

Alternate ingredients, finishing with the apple.

APPLE-GINGER CLEANER

MAKES ABOUT 16 OUNCES

DIGESTION SUPPORT, ANTI-INFLAMMATORY, CLEANSING, HEART HEALTH

1 small lemon
1-inch piece fresh
  ginger root
1 medium apple
1 cup fresh coconut water

Alternate the produce, finishing with the apple. Stir the coconut water directly into the juice.

ORANGE TART

MAKES ABOUT 16 OUNCES

DIGESTION SUPPORT, ANTI-INFLAMMATORY, CLEANSING, HEART HEALTH, IMMUNE SUPPORT, STRUCTURE SUPPORT

2 blood oranges, peeled
1-inch piece fresh
  ginger root
1 large lemon
2 large celery stalks
½ cup fresh
  coconut water

Alternate the produce, finishing with the celery. Stir the coconut water directly into the juice.

TUMMY TAMER

MAKES ABOUT 16 OUNCES

DIGESTION SUPPORT, ANTI-INFLAMMATORY, BRAIN HEALTH, CLEANSING, DETOXIFYING, HEART HEALTH, IMMUNE SUPPORT

2 large celery stalks
½ cup spinach
1 cup papaya
½ firm pear
½-inch piece fresh
   ginger root
4 parsley sprigs
1 large cucumber
¼ cup fresh
   coconut water

Alternate the produce, finishing with the cucumber. Stir the coconut water directly into the juice.

PAPAYA AND PINEAPPLE DIGESTIVE

MAKES ABOUT 16 OUNCES

DIGESTION SUPPORT, ANTI-INFLAMMATORY, CLEANSING, HEART HEALTH, IMMUNE SUPPORT

1 lime, peeled
2 cups papaya
1 cup pineapple
1 cup fresh coconut water

Alternate the produce, finishing with the pineapple. Stir the coconut water directly into the juice.

PAPAYA-PARSLEY REFRESHER

MAKES ABOUT 16 OUNCES

DIGESTION SUPPORT, DETOXIFYING, IMMUNE SUPPORT, MOOD LIFTER

1 lime, peeled
Handful parsley
2 cups papaya
1 small apple

Alternate ingredients, finishing with the apple.

PAPAYA, SPINACH, AND CELERY BLEND

MAKES ABOUT 16 OUNCES

DIGESTION SUPPORT, BRAIN HEALTH, IMMUNE SUPPORT, MOOD LIFTER, STRUCTURE SUPPORT

Handful spinach
2 cups papaya
4 large celery stalks

Alternate ingredients, finishing with the celery.

TROPICAL COCKTAIL

MAKES ABOUT 20 OUNCES

DIGESTION SUPPORT, ANTI-INFLAMMATORY, IMMUNE SUPPORT, STRUCTURE SUPPORT

2 cups papaya
1 cup pineapple
1-inch piece fresh ginger root
1 lime, peeled
4 large celery stalks

Juice the papaya and pineapple first if you want to reserve the pulp for another use. Alternate the remaining ingredients, finishing with the celery.

Pulp Tip: Papaya generally produces a lot of pulp. Freeze the papaya and pineapple pulp for a smoothie or frozen juice pop.

KIWI-PAPAYA PUNCH

MAKES ABOUT 16 OUNCES

DIGESTION SUPPORT, IMMUNE SUPPORT, STRUCTURE SUPPORT

2 cups papaya
4 kiwifruit
2 large celery stalks

Alternate ingredients, finishing with the celery.

QUICK BLOOD ORANGE AND PAPAYA BLEND

MAKES ABOUT 16 OUNCES

DIGESTION SUPPORT, HEART HEALTH, IMMUNE SUPPORT

2 blood oranges, peeled
2 cups papaya
½ cup fresh
  coconut water

Alternate the orange and the papaya. Stir the coconut water directly into the juice.

GRAPEFRUIT AND PAPAYA DIGESTIVE

MAKES ABOUT 16 OUNCES

DIGESTION SUPPORT, IMMUNE SUPPORT, WEIGHT LOSS

1 lime, peeled
2 cups papaya
1 large pink or red
  grapefruit, peeled

Alternate ingredients, finishing with the grapefruit.

GRAPEFRUIT-SPINACH COOLER

MAKES ABOUT 16 OUNCES

DIGESTION SUPPORT, BRAIN HEALTH, STRUCTURE SUPPORT, WEIGHT LOSS

Handful spinach
1 large pink or red
  grapefruit, peeled
1 large cucumber

Alternate ingredients, finishing with the cucumber.

EASY DIGESTION SUPPORT

MAKES ABOUT 16 OUNCES

DIGESTION SUPPORT, BRAIN HEALTH, HEART HEALTH, IMMUNE SUPPORT, MOOD LIFTER

4 small kale leaves
2 large celery stalks
1 cup papaya
1 firm pear
1 small apple

Alternate ingredients, finishing with the apple.

SWEET KALE

MAKES ABOUT 20 OUNCES

DIGESTION SUPPORT, ANTI-INFLAMMATORY, CLEANSING, MOOD LIFTER, STRUCTURE SUPPORT

4 medium kale leaves
1 firm pear
1 cup pineapple
1 large cucumber

Alternate ingredients, finishing with the cucumber.

PINEAPPLE COOLER

MAKES ABOUT 16 OUNCES

DIGESTION SUPPORT, ANTI-INFLAMMATORY, HEART HEALTH, STRUCTURE SUPPORT

1 cup pineapple
1 lime, peeled
1 large cucumber
½ cup fresh
  coconut water

Alternate the produce, finishing with the cucumber.
Stir the coconut water directly into the juice.

PINEAPPLE AND GREEN PEPPER BLEND

MAKES ABOUT 16 OUNCES

DIGESTION SUPPORT, ANTI-INFLAMMATORY, HEART HEALTH, MOOD LIFTER,
STRUCTURE SUPPORT

1 green bell pepper
1 cup pineapple
2 small apples

Alternate ingredients, finishing with the apple.

SWEET WHEATGRASS

MAKES ABOUT 16 OUNCES

DIGESTION SUPPORT, ANTI-INFLAMMATORY, HEART HEALTH, IMMUNE SUPPORT

½ large lemon
4 small apples
1 teaspoon organic
   freeze-dried wheatgrass
   juice powder

Alternate the lemon and the apple, finishing with
the apple. Stir the wheatgrass juice powder directly
into the juice or place the juice and the wheatgrass
juice powder in a jar and shake to combine.

Ingredient Tip: Wheatgrass has traditionally been used to
reduce stomach pain, diarrhea, and other digestive problems.
In a randomized, double-blind, placebo-controlled study,
ulcerative colitis patients receiving wheatgrass juice powder
experienced a significant reduction in disease activity and
symptoms.

PINEAPPLE WHEATGRASS

MAKES ABOUT 20 OUNCES

DIGESTION SUPPORT, ANTI-INFLAMMATORY, IMMUNE SUPPORT, STRUCTURE SUPPORT

2 cups pineapple
1 lime, peeled
4 medium celery stalks
1 teaspoon organic
   freeze-dried wheatgrass
   juice powder

Alternate the produce, finishing with the celery. Stir the wheatgrass juice powder directly into the juice or place the juice and the wheatgrass juice powder in a jar and shake to combine.

TOMATO SALAD

MAKES ABOUT 20 OUNCES

DIGESTION SUPPORT, BRAIN HEALTH, HEART HEALTH, MOOD LIFTER, STRUCTURE SUPPORT

2 cups spinach
1 cup tomato
1 medium lemon
Handful parsley
4 large celery stalks

Alternate ingredients, finishing with the celery.

PINEAPPLE GREENS

MAKES ABOUT 16 OUNCES

DIGESTION SUPPORT, ANTI-INFLAMMATORY, BRAIN HEALTH, MOOD LIFTER, STRUCTURE SUPPORT

4 small kale leaves
4 cups spinach
½ large lemon
1 cup pineapple
1-inch piece fresh
   ginger root
1 large cucumber

Alternate ingredients, finishing with the cucumber.

STROLL ON THE BEACH,
PAGE 99

STROLL ON THE BEACH

MAKES ABOUT 16 OUNCES

DIGESTION SUPPORT, ANTI-INFLAMMATORY, CLEANSING, HEART HEALTH, STRUCTURE SUPPORT

½ green bell pepper
½ large cucumber
½ lime, peeled
1 cup pineapple
1 small apple
½ cup fresh
  coconut water

Alternate the produce, finishing with the apple. Stir the coconut water directly into the juice.

APPLE, PEAR, AND COCONUT BLEND

MAKES ABOUT 16 OUNCES

DIGESTION SUPPORT, CLEANSING, HEART HEALTH

1 firm pear
2 small apples
½ cup fresh
  coconut water

Alternate the pear and the apple, finishing with the apple. Stir the coconut water directly into the juice.

HAPPY MORNING

MAKES ABOUT 16 OUNCES

DIGESTION SUPPORT, IMMUNE SUPPORT, STRUCTURE SUPPORT

3 large carrots
1 cup pineapple
1-inch piece fresh
  ginger root
5 large celery stalks

Alternate ingredients, finishing with the celery.

ASPARAGUS AND SPINACH SALAD

MAKES ABOUT 16 OUNCES

DIGESTION SUPPORT, DETOXIFYING, WEIGHT LOSS

6 asparagus spears
½ large cucumber
Handful spinach
3 small tomatoes (about 1 cup)
1 small lemon
10 parsley sprigs
1 small green or red apple

Alternate ingredients, finishing with the apple.

DEEP PURPLE

MAKES ABOUT 20 OUNCES

DIGESTION SUPPORT, BRAIN HEALTH, HEART HEALTH, MOOD LIFTER, STRUCTURE SUPPORT

4 medium celery stalks
1 cup blackberries
1 medium lemon
2 large romaine leaves
1 large cucumber

Alternate ingredients, finishing with the cucumber.

GRAPES AND WHEATGRASS

DIGESTION SUPPORT, ANTI-INFLAMMATORY, BRAIN HEALTH, CLEANSING, DETOXIFYING, HEART HEALTH, IMMUNE SUPPORT

2 cups black, purple, or red grapes

1 cup fresh coconut water

1 teaspoon organic freeze-dried wheatgrass juice powder

Juice the grapes. Stir the coconut water and wheatgrass juice powder directly into the juice or place the juice, coconut water, and wheatgrass powder in a jar and shake to combine.

PINEAPPLE BOOST,
PAGE 106

CHAPTER 6

HEART
HEALTH

When we talk about heart health, we're really talking about overall cardiovascular health. Juices that benefit the heart also help lower high blood pressure and reduce the risk of stroke and peripheral artery disease. In this chapter, you'll find recipes that include red-orange to blue-violet vegetables and fruits high in anthocyanins, which are associated with a significant reduction in the risk of heart attack and other cardiovascular diseases.

These recipes also focus on vegetables high in nitrates that generate high amounts of nitric oxide. Not to be confused with harmful additives, nitric oxide produced by nitrates found naturally in fresh produce helps arteries relax and expand. Nitric oxide can prevent high blood pressure, keep arteries flexible, and reduce the formation of blood clots. It can also lower cholesterol and prevent, slow, or reverse arterial plaque. High nitric oxide–producing vegetables include kale, Swiss chard, arugula, spinach, radishes, bok choy, beets, lettuce, Chinese cabbage, mustard greens, cauliflower, and broccoli.

HIGH NITRIC OXIDE BOOSTER

MAKES ABOUT 16 OUNCES

HEART HEALTH, BRAIN HEALTH, DETOXIFYING, STRUCTURE SUPPORT, WEIGHT LOSS

Handful arugula

½ medium golden or
  red beet

Handful spinach

3 large carrots

4 cilantro or
  parsley sprigs

1 small lemon

1 medium red apple

Alternate ingredients, finishing with the apple.

NITRIC OXIDE RECHARGE

MAKES ABOUT 20 OUNCES

HEART HEALTH, BRAIN HEALTH, DETOXIFYING, DIGESTION SUPPORT, STRUCTURE SUPPORT, WEIGHT LOSS

Handful arugula

4-inch piece
  broccoli stalk

4 large carrots

1 orange, peeled

4 large celery stalks

Alternate ingredients, finishing with the celery.

SUMMER RUNNER

MAKES ABOUT 16 OUNCES

HEART HEALTH, ANTI-INFLAMMATORY, BRAIN HEALTH, MOOD LIFTER, STRUCTURE SUPPORT

Handful arugula

2 medium kale leaves

2 large carrots

1 red apple

1 cup watermelon

Alternate ingredients, finishing with
the watermelon.

Ingredient Tip: If your watermelon is organic, juice the rind because that is where the amino acid L-citrulline is concentrated. L-citrulline may help lower blood pressure and boost exercise performance.

WELCOMING CARROT

MAKES ABOUT 16 OUNCES

HEART HEALTH, ANTI-INFLAMMATORY, BRAIN HEALTH, DIGESTION SUPPORT, MOOD LIFTER, STRUCTURE SUPPORT

2 large carrots
8 parsley sprigs
1 cup pineapple

Alternate ingredients, finishing with the pineapple.

SPICY PINEAPPLE

MAKES ABOUT 16 OUNCES

HEART HEALTH, ANTI-INFLAMMATORY, BRAIN HEALTH, DETOXIFYING, DIGESTION SUPPORT, STRUCTURE SUPPORT

Handful arugula
3 large carrots
5 large celery stalks
1-inch piece fresh ginger root
1 cup pineapple
½ cup red apple

Alternate ingredients, finishing with the apple.

ARUGULA, CARROT, AND ZUCCHINI BLEND

MAKES ABOUT 20 OUNCES

HEART HEALTH, BRAIN HEALTH, CLEANSING, DETOXIFYING, MOOD LIFTER

Handful arugula
4 medium carrots
1 small zucchini
6 cilantro sprigs
6 parsley sprigs
2 small red apples

Alternate ingredients, finishing with the apple.

Add-in Tip: For increased detoxification support, add 1 teaspoon of chlorella powder directly to the juice. Chlorella powder can be purchased in many grocery stores, in health food stores, or online.

ARUGULA AND CHARD HYDRATOR

MAKES ABOUT 16 OUNCES

HEART HEALTH, BRAIN HEALTH, DETOXIFYING, DIGESTION SUPPORT, MOOD LIFTER, STRUCTURE SUPPORT

Handful arugula
2 large celery stalks
1 large cucumber
Handful kale
¼ lemon
2 cups Swiss chard
2 small red apples

Alternate ingredients, finishing with the apple.

PINEAPPLE BOOST

MAKES ABOUT 16 OUNCES

HEART HEALTH, ANTI-INFLAMMATORY, BRAIN HEALTH, DETOXIFYING, DIGESTION SUPPORT, MOOD LIFTER, STRUCTURE SUPPORT

Handful arugula
4 small kale leaves
2 cups spinach
½ lemon
1-inch piece fresh
  ginger root
1 cup pineapple
1 cucumber

Alternate ingredients, finishing with the cucumber.

CHARD, CABBAGE, AND PEAR COOLER

MAKES ABOUT 16 OUNCES

HEART HEALTH, BRAIN HEALTH, CLEANSING, DIGESTION SUPPORT, MOOD LIFTER, WEIGHT LOSS

1 cup red cabbage
2 large Swiss chard leaves
1 firm red pear
4 medium romaine leaves

Alternate ingredients, finishing with the romaine.

GRAPE-APPLE GREENS

MAKES ABOUT 16 OUNCES

HEART HEALTH, ANTI-INFLAMMATORY, BRAIN HEALTH, DETOXIFYING, DIGESTION SUPPORT, MOOD LIFTER

2 cups black, purple, or
   red grapes
3 large celery stalks
2 large romaine leaves
Handful spinach
½ lime, peeled
2 small red apples

Alternate ingredients, finishing with the apple.

BERRY, BEET, AND BOK CHOY BLEND

MAKES ABOUT 16 OUNCES

HEART HEALTH, BRAIN HEALTH, DETOXIFYING, MOOD LIFTER, STRUCTURE SUPPORT, WEIGHT LOSS

1 cup raspberries
8 medium
   asparagus spears
1 medium golden or
   red beet
1 large bok choy stem
4 large romaine leaves
1 large celery stalk

Alternate ingredients, finishing with the celery.

CAULIFLOWER CARDIO COCKTAIL

MAKES ABOUT 16 OUNCES

HEART HEALTH, BRAIN HEALTH, DETOXIFYING, DIGESTION SUPPORT, MOOD LIFTER, STRUCTURE SUPPORT

1 cup cauliflower
2 large celery stalks
8 parsley sprigs
2 small red apples
½ cucumber

Alternate ingredients, finishing with the cucumber.

HIGH SUMMER SIPPER

MAKES ABOUT 20 OUNCES

HEART HEALTH, ANTI-INFLAMMATORY, BRAIN HEALTH, MOOD LIFTER, STRUCTURE SUPPORT

4 romaine leaves
1 small red apple
1 orange, peeled
1 cup raspberries
1 cup watermelon
½ cup cucumber

Alternate ingredients, finishing with the cucumber.

PAPAYA-BERRY COCKTAIL

MAKES ABOUT 16 OUNCES

HEART HEALTH, ANTI-INFLAMMATORY, BRAIN HEALTH, DIGESTION SUPPORT, IMMUNE SUPPORT, MOOD LIFTER

1 cup papaya
1 cup raspberries
1 cup watermelon
4 large romaine leaves
1 red apple
1 large celery stalk

Alternate ingredients, finishing with the celery.

RASPBERRY LIMEADE

MAKES ABOUT 16 OUNCES

HEART HEALTH, ANTI-INFLAMMATORY, BRAIN HEALTH, IMMUNE SUPPORT

1 cup raspberries
2 medium red apples
1 lime, peeled
2 cups watermelon

Alternate ingredients, finishing with the watermelon.

TART APPLE AND MINT REFRESHER

MAKES ABOUT 20 OUNCES

HEART HEALTH, ANTI-INFLAMMATORY, BRAIN HEALTH

1 red apple
½ large lemon
16 fresh mint leaves
2 cups watermelon

Alternate ingredients, finishing with
the watermelon.

ORANGE, SPINACH, AND BEET BLEND

MAKES ABOUT 24 OUNCES

HEART HEALTH, BRAIN HEALTH, DIGESTION SUPPORT, IMMUNE SUPPORT, MOOD LIFTER,
STRUCTURE SUPPORT, WEIGHT LOSS

1 medium golden or
  red beet

Handful spinach
½ lemon
1 large orange, peeled
1 large cucumber

Alternate ingredients, finishing with the cucumber.

BERRY CITRUS BEET

MAKES ABOUT 16 OUNCES

HEART HEALTH, BRAIN HEALTH, DIGESTION SUPPORT, IMMUNE SUPPORT, MOOD LIFTER,
STRUCTURE SUPPORT

1 cup raspberries
1 medium golden or
  red beet
1 orange, peeled
2 large celery stalks

Alternate ingredients, finishing with the celery.

GRAPES AND GREENS

MAKES ABOUT 16 OUNCES

HEART HEALTH, ANTI-INFLAMMATORY, BRAIN HEALTH, DETOXIFYING, DIGESTION SUPPORT, STRUCTURE SUPPORT

1 cup black, purple, or
   red grapes

1 cup raspberries

2 cups mixed greens

2 large celery stalks

1 large cucumber

Alternate ingredients, finishing with the cucumber.

Ingredient Tip: Although the thick stems of the mature versions of leafy greens provide more yield and may be more cost-effective, large tubs of triple-washed mixed green blends that include baby spinach, kale, and Swiss chard are a convenient, easy way to get a variety of greens into your juice.

KIWI, GRAPES, AND GREENS BLEND

MAKES ABOUT 16 OUNCES

HEART HEALTH, ANTI-INFLAMMATORY, BRAIN HEALTH, DETOXIFYING, DIGESTION SUPPORT, IMMUNE SUPPORT, MOOD LIFTER, STRUCTURE SUPPORT

1 cup black, purple, or
   red grapes

2 kiwifruit

½ lemon

Handful mixed greens

1 large celery stalk

Alternate ingredients, finishing with the celery.

RASPBERRY-CAULI COOLER

MAKES ABOUT 16 OUNCES

HEART HEALTH, BRAIN HEALTH, DETOXIFYING, DIGESTION SUPPORT, STRUCTURE SUPPORT

1 cup raspberries

1 cup cauliflower

1 large celery stalk

½ lemon

1 large cucumber

Alternate ingredients, finishing with the cucumber.

FENNEL AND FRIENDS

MAKES ABOUT 16 OUNCES

HEART HEALTH, BRAIN HEALTH, DETOXIFYING

½ cup cauliflower
½ medium fennel bulb
½ large celery stalk
¼ lemon
1 small blood
   orange, peeled
1 medium red apple
¼ large cucumber

Alternate ingredients, finishing with the cucumber.

VERY RASPBERRY GREENS

MAKES ABOUT 16 OUNCES

HEART HEALTH, BRAIN HEALTH, DIGESTION SUPPORT, IMMUNE SUPPORT, MOOD LIFTER, STRUCTURE SUPPORT

1 cup raspberries
2 cups mixed greens
1 firm red pear
2 small blood
   oranges, peeled

Alternate ingredients, finishing with the orange.

FRUITY CAULI COOLER

MAKES ABOUT 16 OUNCES

HEART HEALTH, BRAIN HEALTH, CLEANSING, DIGESTION SUPPORT, MOOD LIFTER, STRUCTURE SUPPORT

½ cup cauliflower
½ cup raspberries
Handful mixed greens
1 firm red pear
1 small red apple
½ large cucumber

Alternate ingredients, finishing with the cucumber.

KIWI-KALE COCKTAIL

MAKES ABOUT 16 OUNCES

HEART HEALTH, ANTI-INFLAMMATORY, BRAIN HEALTH, DETOXIFYING, MOOD LIFTER, STRUCTURE SUPPORT

½ cup black, purple, or red grapes

2 kiwifruit

4 medium kale leaves

½ large cucumber

Alternate ingredients, finishing with the cucumber.

HAPPY HEART

MAKES ABOUT 16 OUNCES

HEART HEALTH, BRAIN HEALTH, CLEANSING, DETOXIFYING, DIGESTION SUPPORT, MOOD LIFTER

1 medium collard leaf

2 firm red pears

½ lemon

½ large cucumber

Alternate ingredients, finishing with the cucumber.

RED KALE IN SUMMER

MAKES ABOUT 16 OUNCES

HEART HEALTH, ANTI-INFLAMMATORY, BRAIN HEALTH, DETOXIFYING, MOOD LIFTER, STRUCTURE SUPPORT

1 cup black, purple, or red grapes

4 small red kale leaves

2 cups watermelon

Alternate ingredients, finishing with the watermelon.

WATERMELON-PEAR COOLER

MAKES ABOUT 16 OUNCES

HEART HEALTH, ANTI-INFLAMMATORY, BRAIN HEALTH, CLEANSING, DIGESTION SUPPORT

1 firm red pear
2 cups watermelon
½ cup fresh
  coconut water

Alternate the pear and the watermelon, finishing with the watermelon. Stir the coconut water directly into the juice.

SWEET HEART

MAKES ABOUT 16 OUNCES

HEART HEALTH, ANTI-INFLAMMATORY, BRAIN HEALTH, CLEANSING, DETOXIFYING, DIGESTION SUPPORT

2 small kale leaves
½ cup black, purple, or
  red grapes
½ firm red pear
2 cups watermelon
¼ cup fresh coconut
  water (optional)

Alternate the produce, finishing with the watermelon. Stir the coconut water (if using) directly into the juice.

COLLARDS IN THE SUN

MAKES ABOUT 16 OUNCES

HEART HEALTH, ANTI-INFLAMMATORY, BRAIN HEALTH, DETOXIFYING, IMMUNE SUPPORT, MOOD LIFTER

1 medium collard leaf
½ lemon
1 cup mango
2 cups watermelon
½ cup fresh
  coconut water

Alternate the produce, finishing with the watermelon. Stir the coconut water directly into the juice.

TOMATO-WATERMELON SALAD

MAKES ABOUT 24 OUNCES

HEART HEALTH, ANTI-INFLAMMATORY, BRAIN HEALTH, DIGESTION SUPPORT

2 large celery stalks
½ cucumber
1 cup tomato
½ lemon
3 cups watermelon

Alternate ingredients, finishing with the watermelon.

SWISS WATERMELON

MAKES ABOUT 20 OUNCES

HEART HEALTH, ANTI-INFLAMMATORY, BRAIN HEALTH, DETOXIFYING, MOOD LIFTER, STRUCTURE SUPPORT

2 cups Swiss chard
1 large cucumber
½ lemon
2 cups watermelon

Alternate ingredients, finishing with the watermelon.

STRONG HEART

MAKES ABOUT 20 OUNCES

HEART HEALTH, ANTI-INFLAMMATORY, BRAIN HEALTH, CLEANSING, DETOXIFYING, MOOD LIFTER, STRUCTURE SUPPORT

1 small collard leaf
1 cup red Swiss chard
½ lemon
¼ lime, peeled
½ mango
2 cups watermelon
½ cucumber
¼ to ½ cup fresh coconut water

Alternate the produce, finishing with the cucumber. Stir the coconut water directly into the juice.

WATERMELON, FENNEL, AND KALE BLEND

MAKES ABOUT 14 OUNCES

HEART HEALTH, ANTI-INFLAMMATORY, BRAIN HEALTH, DETOXIFYING, MOOD LIFTER

2 cups fennel
4 medium kale leaves
4 cups watermelon

Alternate ingredients, finishing with the watermelon.

PEAR, WATERMELON, AND COLLARDS COOLER

MAKES ABOUT 16 OUNCES

HEART HEALTH, ANTI-INFLAMMATORY, BRAIN HEALTH, CLEANSING, DIGESTION SUPPORT, MOOD LIFTER

1 medium collard leaf
¼ lime, peeled
½ firm red pear
1 cup watermelon
½ cup fresh
   coconut water

Alternate the produce, finishing with the watermelon. Stir the coconut water directly into the juice.

SWEET CABBAGE HEART HELPER

MAKES ABOUT 16 OUNCES

HEART HEALTH, ANTI-INFLAMMATORY, BRAIN HEALTH, DIGESTION SUPPORT

1 cup red cabbage
1 medium red apple
2 cups watermelon

Alternate ingredients, finishing with the watermelon.

BOK CHOY AND TOMATO BLEND

MAKES ABOUT 16 OUNCES

HEART HEALTH, BRAIN HEALTH, DETOXIFYING, MOOD LIFTER

Handful parsley
½ medium lemon
4 small orange or
 purple carrots
1 cup tomato
2 large bok choy stems

Alternate ingredients, finishing with the bok choy.

HEART BEET

MAKES ABOUT 16 OUNCES

HEART HEALTH, BRAIN HEALTH, CLEANSING, DETOXIFYING, DIGESTION SUPPORT, MOOD LIFTER

1 medium golden or
 red beet
1 firm red pear
1 cup cauliflower
4 large celery stalks

Alternate ingredients, finishing with the celery.

CRANBERRY-CARROT COCKTAIL

MAKES ABOUT 16 OUNCES

HEART HEALTH, ANTI-INFLAMMATORY, BRAIN HEALTH, DETOXIFYING, IMMUNE SUPPORT, MOOD LIFTER

2 cups fresh cranberries
2 large carrots
2 large kale leaves
1-inch piece fresh
 ginger root
1 medium red apple
1 orange, peeled

Alternate ingredients, finishing with the orange.

PINEAPPLE-CRANBERRY COCKTAIL

MAKES ABOUT 24 OUNCES

HEART HEALTH, ANTI-INFLAMMATORY, BRAIN HEALTH, IMMUNE SUPPORT

1 cup fresh cranberries
1-inch piece fresh ginger root
2 medium red apples
1 cup pineapple
2 oranges, peeled

Alternate ingredients, finishing with the orange.

MOUNTAINEER

MAKES ABOUT 16 OUNCES

HEART HEALTH, BRAIN HEALTH, DETOXIFYING, MOOD LIFTER, STRUCTURE SUPPORT

Handful arugula
1 medium golden or red beet
½ red bell pepper
2 medium red apples
½ large cucumber

Alternate ingredients, finishing with the cucumber.

PRE-RUN HYDRATOR

MAKES ABOUT 16 OUNCES

HEART HEALTH, BRAIN HEALTH, DETOXIFYING, DIGESTION SUPPORT, MOOD LIFTER

1 medium golden or red beet
2-inch piece broccoli stem
2 large celery stalks
½ lemon
1 large cucumber

Alternate ingredients, finishing with the cucumber.

HEALTHY AND HAPPY,
PAGE 119

HEALTHY AND HAPPY

MAKES ABOUT 16 OUNCES

HEART HEALTH, BRAIN HEALTH, DETOXIFYING, DIGESTION SUPPORT, MOOD LIFTER, STRUCTURE SUPPORT

1 medium golden or
  red beet
½ red bell pepper
1 cup red cabbage
1 medium red apple
1 cucumber

Alternate ingredients, finishing with the cucumber.

SPICY MANGO

MAKES ABOUT 16 OUNCES

HEART HEALTH, BRAIN HEALTH, DETOXIFYING, DIGESTION SUPPORT, MOOD LIFTER

1 cup mango
1 red apple
1 small mustard green leaf
3 large celery stalks

Juice the mango and the apple first if you want to reserve the pulp for another use. Alternate the remaining ingredients, finishing with the celery.

Pulp Tip: Use the mango and apple pulp as a spread for toast.

VEGGIE GOODNESS

MAKES ABOUT 16 OUNCES

HEART HEALTH, BRAIN HEALTH, IMMUNE SUPPORT, MOOD LIFTER, STRUCTURE SUPPORT, WEIGHT LOSS

1 large carrot
8 parsley sprigs
½ medium lemon
Handful mixed greens
1 red bell pepper

Alternate ingredients, finishing with the bell pepper.

Pulp Tip: If you have a dehydrator, use the pulp to make juice pulp crackers. Combine 1½ to 2 cups of juice pulp with ¼ cup of nutritional yeast, ¼ cup of ground flaxseed, 3 to 4 tablespoons of coconut aminos, and ¼ teaspoon of black pepper in a food processor. Pulse until combined, adding 1 to 2 tablespoons of water, if necessary. Transfer the pulp to a dehydrator sheet and spread to ⅛ to ¼ inch thick. Score into cracker-size pieces. Dehydrate for 4 to 5 hours at 115°F to 120°F. Flip and dehydrate for another 4 hours, or until dry and crispy.

RED CABBAGE COOLER

MAKES ABOUT 16 OUNCES

HEART HEALTH, ANTI-INFLAMMATORY, BRAIN HEALTH, DIGESTION SUPPORT

½ red bell pepper
1 cup red cabbage
2 large celery stalks
2 cups watermelon

Alternate ingredients, finishing with the watermelon.

POM-ORANGE GREENS

MAKES ABOUT 16 OUNCES

HEART HEALTH, BRAIN HEALTH, DIGESTION SUPPORT, IMMUNE SUPPORT, MOOD LIFTER, STRUCTURE SUPPORT

Handful mixed greens
4 large celery stalks
4 small blood oranges or other oranges, peeled
2 teaspoons freeze-dried pomegranate juice powder

Alternate the produce, finishing with the orange or the celery. Stir the pomegranate juice powder directly into the juice or place the juice and the pomegranate juice powder in a jar and shake to combine.

Ingredient Tip: Fresh pomegranates are only available for a few weeks each season. Freeze-dried pomegranate juice powder makes it possible to get the blood pressure–reducing and cholesterol-lowering benefits year-round.

CITRUSY SUPER GREENS

MAKES ABOUT 20 OUNCES

HEART HEALTH, BRAIN HEALTH, DETOXIFYING, IMMUNE SUPPORT, MOOD LIFTER

12 sprigs parsley
4 large bok choy stems
4 small blood oranges or other oranges, peeled
1 teaspoon Vitamineral Green or organic freeze-dried wheatgrass juice powder

Alternate the produce, finishing with the orange or the bok choy. Stir the Vitamineral Green directly into the juice or place the juice and the Vitamineral Green in a jar and shake to combine.

Ingredient Tip: A superfood greens blend like Vitamineral Green is an easy way to add a wide range of beneficial grasses, algae, and sea vegetables to your diet. You can find it at some grocery stores and most health food stores or online at HealthForceSuperFoods.com and other online retailers.

STRAWBERRY FENNEL

MAKES ABOUT 16 OUNCES

HEART HEALTH, BRAIN HEALTH, IMMUNE SUPPORT, MOOD LIFTER, STRUCTURE SUPPORT

1 small fennel bulb
1 cup strawberries
2 cups mixed greens
2 small red apples

Alternate ingredients, finishing with the apple.

BELL PEPPER AND BOK CHOY BLEND

MAKES ABOUT 20 OUNCES

HEART HEALTH, BRAIN HEALTH, DETOXIFYING, IMMUNE SUPPORT, MOOD LIFTER

2 red bell peppers
2 large bok choy stems
½ medium lemon
1 small red apple

Alternate ingredients, finishing with the apple.

STRAWBERRY, KIWI, AND COLLARD COCKTAIL

MAKES ABOUT 16 OUNCES

HEART HEALTH, BRAIN HEALTH, DETOXIFYING, IMMUNE SUPPORT, MOOD LIFTER

2 large celery stalks
1 medium collard leaf
1 kiwifruit
1 cup strawberries
1 red apple

Alternate ingredients, finishing with the apple.

GREENS AND REDS

MAKES ABOUT 16 OUNCES

HEART HEALTH, BRAIN HEALTH, IMMUNE SUPPORT, MOOD LIFTER, STRUCTURE SUPPORT

Handful mixed greens
1 cup strawberries
1 cup tomato
1 kiwifruit
1 red apple

Alternate ingredients, finishing with the apple.

MIXED BERRY AND BOK CHOY

MAKES ABOUT 16 OUNCES

HEART HEALTH, BRAIN HEALTH, DETOXIFYING, MOOD LIFTER, STRUCTURE SUPPORT, WEIGHT LOSS

2 large bok choy stems
1 cup mixed berries
Handful mixed greens
½ medium red apple
¼ medium lemon
½ large cucumber

Alternate ingredients, finishing with the cucumber.

SQUASH SPLASH

MAKES ABOUT 24 OUNCES

HEART HEALTH, BRAIN HEALTH, MOOD LIFTER, STRUCTURE SUPPORT

4 medium orange or
   purple carrots

1 cup butternut squash or
   other winter squash

1 medium lemon

2 small red apples

1 large cucumber

Alternate ingredients, finishing with the cucumber.

PURPLE POTATO PUNCH

MAKES ABOUT 16 OUNCES

HEART HEALTH, BRAIN HEALTH, MOOD LIFTER, STRUCTURE SUPPORT

1 cup peeled Stokes
   Purple sweet potato

2 small red apples

1 medium lemon

1 large cucumber

Alternate ingredients, finishing with the cucumber.

Ingredient Tip: The deep purple flesh of a Stokes Purple sweet potato is high in anthocyanins, the same flavonoid pigment found in blueberries that's associated with a reduced risk of cardiovascular disease. Visit Friedas.com/where-to-buy to locate a store near you that has this sweet potato in stock.

PURPLE ROOTS

MAKES ABOUT 16 OUNCES

HEART HEALTH, BRAIN HEALTH, MOOD LIFTER, STRUCTURE SUPPORT

1 cup peeled Stokes
   Purple sweet potato

8 medium carrots

1 medium red apple

1 large cucumber

Alternate ingredients, finishing with the cucumber.

GOLDEN HEART BEET JUICE

MAKES ABOUT 16 OUNCES

HEART HEALTH, BRAIN HEALTH, IMMUNE SUPPORT

6 medium carrots
¼ lemon
1 orange, peeled
½ golden or red beet
1 medium red apple

Alternate ingredients, finishing with the apple.

Ingredient Tip: Golden or yellow beets provide nutrition similar to red beets but with a milder taste and less staining.

APPLE SALAD

MAKES ABOUT 12 OUNCES

HEART HEALTH, BONE HEALTH, DIGESTION SUPPORT, WEIGHT LOSS

2 large celery stalks
4 large kale leaves
4 large romaine leaves
1 red apple

Alternate ingredients, finishing with the apple.

SPICY ROOTS

MAKES ABOUT 16 OUNCES

HEART HEALTH, ANTI-INFLAMMATORY, BRAIN HEALTH, MOOD LIFTER, STRUCTURE SUPPORT, WEIGHT LOSS

Handful arugula
1 red bell pepper
**1-inch piece fresh
    ginger root**
4 large carrots
1 small red apple

Alternate ingredients, finishing with the apple.

RASPBERRY-APPLE SALAD

MAKES ABOUT 16 OUNCES

HEART HEALTH, BRAIN HEALTH, DETOXIFYING, DIGESTION SUPPORT, MOOD LIFTER, WEIGHT LOSS

Handful arugula
1 cup raspberries
4 small celery stalks
4 medium kale leaves
2 large romaine leaves
12 parsley sprigs
1 small red apple

Alternate ingredients, finishing with the apple.

ROSY CARROT,
PAGE 131

CHAPTER 7

IMMUNITY BOOST

A micronutrient-rich diet is the key to a healthy immune system that can fend off toxins, infections, and cancer development, as well as protect you from auto-immune diseases. Fresh fruit and vegetable juices are a fun and delicious way to get these critical vitamins, minerals, and phytonutrients into your diet.

The recipes in this chapter focus on produce high in vitamin C, vitamin A, and folate. This includes citrus fruits and melon, as well as colorful bell peppers. (I recommend yellow for immune support, but you can use any color.) Cruciferous greens and berries are included because they have been shown to significantly reduce the risk of cancer. The falcarinol in carrots and the luteolin and apigenin in celery are also powerful anticancer compounds. Pears, apples, grapes, and pine-apple are other anticancer fruits. Cucumbers and sweet potatoes round out the cancer-protective vegetables.

In addition to getting lots of produce into your diet, for a robust immune system, ensure you are getting adequate amounts of vitamin D and B$_{12}$, through supplementation if necessary. Try to get adequate sleep, exercise, manage your stress, and avoid drinking too much alcohol. Enjoy a fresh juice instead!

SUMMER STROLL

MAKES ABOUT 16 OUNCES

IMMUNE SUPPORT, ANTI-INFLAMMATORY, BRAIN HEALTH, HEART HEALTH, MOOD LIFTER, STRUCTURE SUPPORT

2 large celery stalks
1 medium kale leaf
2 kiwifruit
1 small lime, peeled
1 cup pineapple
1 cup watermelon

Alternate ingredients, finishing with the watermelon.

ORANGE, MELON, AND BERRY BLEND

MAKES ABOUT 20 OUNCES

IMMUNE SUPPORT, ANTI-INFLAMMATORY, BRAIN HEALTH, DIGESTION SUPPORT, HEART HEALTH, MOOD LIFTER, STRUCTURE SUPPORT

1 cup strawberries
2 large romaine leaves
½ cup spinach
1 large celery stalk
2 oranges, peeled
1 cup watermelon

Alternate ingredients, finishing with the watermelon.

GREAT START

MAKES ABOUT 12 OUNCES

IMMUNE SUPPORT, BRAIN HEALTH, HEART HEALTH, STRUCTURE SUPPORT

3 medium carrots
2 small oranges, peeled

Alternate ingredients, finishing with the orange.

DOUBLE C

MAKES ABOUT 16 OUNCES

IMMUNE SUPPORT, DETOXIFYING, MOOD LIFTER, STRUCTURE SUPPORT, WEIGHT LOSS

2 medium collard leaves
1 grapefruit, peeled
2 small oranges, peeled

Alternate ingredients, finishing with the orange.

FRUIT SALAD

MAKES ABOUT 16 OUNCES

IMMUNE SUPPORT, ANTI-INFLAMMATORY, BRAIN HEALTH, DIGESTION SUPPORT, HEART HEALTH

1 large celery stalk
4 large romaine leaves
1 small apple
1 cup papaya
1 cup strawberries
1 cup watermelon

Alternate ingredients, finishing with the watermelon.

SWEET SUMMER KALE

MAKES ABOUT 16 OUNCES

IMMUNE SUPPORT, ANTI-INFLAMMATORY, DETOXIFYING, DIGESTION SUPPORT, MOOD LIFTER, STRUCTURE SUPPORT

2 large kale leaves
½ cup black, purple, or red grapes
½ cup pineapple
2 cups watermelon

Alternate ingredients, finishing with the watermelon.

KALE IN PARADISE

MAKES ABOUT 16 OUNCES

IMMUNE SUPPORT, CLEANSING, DIGESTION SUPPORT, HEART HEALTH, MOOD LIFTER, STRUCTURE SUPPORT

1 large kale leaf
1 cup mango
½ lime, peeled
2 cups watermelon
½ cup fresh
   coconut water

Alternate the produce, finishing with the watermelon. Stir the coconut water directly into the juice.

GRAPEFRUIT SALAD

MAKES ABOUT 16 OUNCES

IMMUNE SUPPORT, DIGESTION SUPPORT, MOOD LIFTER, STRUCTURE SUPPORT, WEIGHT LOSS

2 large celery stalks
4 large romaine leaves
1 pink or red
   grapefruit, peeled

Alternate ingredients, finishing with the grapefruit.

SUNNY SPINACH

MAKES ABOUT 20 OUNCES

IMMUNE SUPPORT, ANTI-INFLAMMATORY, HEART HEALTH, MOOD LIFTER, STRUCTURE SUPPORT, WEIGHT LOSS

4 cups spinach
½ pink or red
   grapefruit, peeled
4 cups watermelon

Alternate ingredients, finishing with the watermelon.

SIMPLE PLEASURES

MAKES ABOUT 16 OUNCES

IMMUNE SUPPORT, ANTI-INFLAMMATORY, HEART HEALTH, STRUCTURE SUPPORT, WEIGHT LOSS

1 pink or red
  grapefruit, peeled
2 cups watermelon

Alternate ingredients, finishing with
the watermelon.

MELON 'N' LIME

MAKES ABOUT 16 OUNCES

IMMUNE SUPPORT, STRUCTURE SUPPORT

2 limes, peeled
4 cups cantaloupe

Alternate ingredients, finishing with the cantaloupe.

ROSY CARROT

MAKES ABOUT 16 OUNCES

IMMUNE SUPPORT, HEART HEALTH, STRUCTURE SUPPORT

4 medium carrots
1 cup cantaloupe

Alternate ingredients, finishing with the cantaloupe.

GREEN DRAGON QUEEN

MAKES ABOUT 16 OUNCES

IMMUNE SUPPORT, BONE HEALTH, STRUCTURE SUPPORT, WEIGHT LOSS

1 dragon fruit (pitaya)
1 small collard leaf
1 large cucumber
Handful spinach
1 small apple

Cut open the dragon fruit, scoop out the pulp and
seeds, and discard the rind. Alternate ingredients,
finishing with the apple.

Ingredient Tip: Dragon fruit season is early summer through
early fall. If you can't find dragon fruit at your grocery store,
you can use 1 to 2 kiwifruit and ½ of a firm pear instead.

BELL PEPPER AND MELON IMMUNE BOOSTER

MAKES ABOUT 20 OUNCES

IMMUNE SUPPORT, BRAIN HEALTH, HEART HEALTH, MOOD LIFTER, STRUCTURE SUPPORT

1 large yellow bell pepper
4 cups watermelon

Alternate ingredients, finishing with the watermelon.

Ingredient Tip: In this chapter, you'll see yellow bell peppers prioritized over orange or red because they have the highest amount of vitamin C. One large yellow bell pepper delivers about 341 mg of vitamin C, while a red pepper provides 209 mg.

ORANGE-MANGO MORNING

MAKES ABOUT 16 OUNCES

IMMUNE SUPPORT, ANTI-INFLAMMATORY, STRUCTURE SUPPORT

1 cup mango
1-inch piece fresh
   ginger root
2 oranges, peeled
½ large cucumber

Alternate ingredients, finishing with the cucumber.

TROPICAL ARUGULA BOOST

MAKES ABOUT 20 OUNCES

IMMUNE SUPPORT, ANTI-INFLAMMATORY, DETOXIFYING, DIGESTION SUPPORT, HEART HEALTH, STRUCTURE SUPPORT

Handful arugula
1-inch piece fresh
   ginger root
1 lime, peeled
1 cup mango
1 orange, peeled
1 cup papaya
½ large cucumber

Alternate ingredients, finishing with the cucumber.

HIGH-C PEAR

MAKES ABOUT 16 OUNCES

IMMUNE SUPPORT, ANTI-INFLAMMATORY, DIGESTION SUPPORT, STRUCTURE SUPPORT

1 orange, peeled
1 cup papaya
1 firm pear
1-inch piece fresh
ginger root
½ large cucumber

Alternate ingredients, finishing with the cucumber.

KALIN' IT

MAKES ABOUT 16 OUNCES

IMMUNE SUPPORT, BRAIN HEALTH, DETOXIFYING, HEART HEALTH, MOOD LIFTER, STRUCTURE SUPPORT

Handful arugula
½ yellow bell pepper
4 small kale leaves
1 cup black, purple, or
red grapes
1 orange, peeled

Alternate ingredients, finishing with the orange.

CAULIFLOWER POWER

MAKES ABOUT 16 OUNCES

IMMUNE SUPPORT, BRAIN HEALTH, DETOXIFYING, DIGESTION SUPPORT, HEART HEALTH, MOOD LIFTER, STRUCTURE SUPPORT

½ cup cauliflower
4 large celery stalks
2 cups watermelon

Alternate ingredients, finishing with the watermelon.

BELL PEPPER AND SPINACH BLEND

MAKES ABOUT 16 OUNCES

IMMUNE SUPPORT, BRAIN HEALTH, DIGESTION SUPPORT, HEART HEALTH, MOOD LIFTER, STRUCTURE SUPPORT, WEIGHT LOSS

2 large yellow
   bell peppers
4 cups spinach
1 lemon
½ large cucumber

Alternate ingredients, finishing with the cucumber.

STRAWBERRY, MANGO, AND KIWI COOLER

MAKES ABOUT 16 OUNCES

IMMUNE SUPPORT, ANTI-INFLAMMATORY, BRAIN HEALTH, DIGESTION SUPPORT, HEART HEALTH, STRUCTURE SUPPORT

2 cups kiwifruit
2 cups mango
1 cup strawberries
1-inch piece fresh
   ginger root
4 medium celery stalks

Alternate ingredients, finishing with the celery.

Pulp Tip: Reserve the fruit pulp for a smoothie or frozen juice pop.

KIWI, ORANGE, AND GINGER KICKER

MAKES ABOUT 16 OUNCES

IMMUNE SUPPORT, ANTI-INFLAMMATORY, BRAIN HEALTH, HEART HEALTH, MOOD LIFTER, STRUCTURE SUPPORT

1 large yellow bell pepper
2-inch piece fresh
   ginger root
2 kiwifruit
2 oranges, peeled

Alternate ingredients, finishing with the orange.

ORCHARD KIWI

MAKES ABOUT 16 OUNCES

IMMUNE SUPPORT, CLEANSING, DIGESTION SUPPORT, HEART HEALTH, STRUCTURE SUPPORT

2 kiwifruit
2 firm pears
½ large cucumber

Alternate ingredients, finishing with the cucumber.

MELON MANGO TANGO

MAKES ABOUT 16 OUNCES

IMMUNE SUPPORT, HEART HEALTH, STRUCTURE SUPPORT

2 kiwifruit
1 lemon
1 cup mango
2 cups cantaloupe

Alternate ingredients, finishing with the cantaloupe.

CARROT, KIWI, AND GINGER KICKER

MAKES ABOUT 16 OUNCES

IMMUNE SUPPORT, ANTI-INFLAMMATORY, HEART HEALTH, STRUCTURE SUPPORT

2-inch piece fresh
   ginger root
4 kiwifruit
1 lemon
8 medium carrots

Alternate ingredients, finishing with the carrot.

ORANGE SUNRISE

MAKES ABOUT 16 OUNCES

IMMUNE SUPPORT, BRAIN HEALTH, DIGESTION SUPPORT, HEART HEALTH, MOOD LIFTER, STRUCTURE SUPPORT

1 large yellow bell pepper
2 kiwifruit
1 cup papaya
1 orange, peeled

Alternate ingredients, finishing with the orange.

STRAWBERRY, CITRUS, AND BOK CHOY BLEND

MAKES ABOUT 16 OUNCES

IMMUNE SUPPORT, BRAIN HEALTH, DETOXIFYING, HEART HEALTH, STRUCTURE SUPPORT, WEIGHT LOSS

2 large bok choy stems
½ pink or red
    grapefruit, peeled
1 cup strawberries
1 orange, peeled

Alternate ingredients, finishing with the orange.

MELON, PAPAYA, AND KIWI BLEND

MAKES ABOUT 16 OUNCES

IMMUNE SUPPORT, DIGESTION SUPPORT, HEART HEALTH, STRUCTURE SUPPORT

2 cups papaya
2 kiwifruit
1 lime, peeled
2 cups cantaloupe

Alternate ingredients, finishing with the cantaloupe.

BROCCOLI TREAT

MAKES ABOUT 20 OUNCES

IMMUNE SUPPORT, ANTI-INFLAMMATORY, BRAIN HEALTH, DETOXIFYING, DIGESTION SUPPORT, HEART HEALTH

½ cup broccoli stems
1 cup pineapple
4 cups watermelon

Alternate ingredients, finishing with the watermelon.

BERRY-CITRUS GARDEN

MAKES ABOUT 20 OUNCES

IMMUNE SUPPORT, BRAIN HEALTH, HEART HEALTH, MOOD LIFTER, STRUCTURE SUPPORT, WEIGHT LOSS

½ large yellow bell pepper
1 pink or red
  grapefruit, peeled
2 cups strawberries
½ large cucumber

Alternate ingredients, finishing with the cucumber.

PINEAPPLE AND GREENS

MAKES ABOUT 16 OUNCES

IMMUNE SUPPORT, BRAIN HEALTH, DETOXIFYING, HEART HEALTH, STRUCTURE SUPPORT, WEIGHT LOSS

½ cup arugula
2 medium kale leaves
1 orange, peeled
2 cups pineapple

Alternate ingredients, finishing with the pineapple or the orange.

ORANGE-GINGER SHOT

MAKES 2 TO 3 OUNCES

IMMUNE SUPPORT, ANTI-INFLAMMATORY, DIGESTION SUPPORT, HEART HEALTH, STRUCTURE SUPPORT

½- to 1-inch piece fresh ginger root

1 small orange, peeled

Alternate ingredients, finishing with the orange.

BELL PEPPER AND GINGER SHOT

MAKES ABOUT 2 OUNCES

IMMUNE SUPPORT, ANTI-INFLAMMATORY, DIGESTION SUPPORT, STRUCTURE SUPPORT

½- to 1-inch piece fresh ginger root

¼ large yellow bell pepper

¼ lemon

2-inch piece celery

Alternate ingredients, finishing with the celery.

BELL PEPPER BOOST

MAKES ABOUT 24 OUNCES

IMMUNE SUPPORT, ANTI-INFLAMMATORY, MOOD LIFTER, STRUCTURE SUPPORT, WEIGHT LOSS

2 large yellow bell peppers

1 large celery stalk

1 lemon

1-inch piece fresh ginger root

1 pink or red grapefruit, peeled

Alternate ingredients, finishing with the grapefruit.

PINEAPPLE-GRAPEFRUIT COOLER

MAKES ABOUT 16 OUNCES

IMMUNE SUPPORT, ANTI-INFLAMMATORY, CLEANSING, DIGESTION SUPPORT, STRUCTURE SUPPORT, WEIGHT LOSS

4 medium celery stalks
½ large cucumber
Handful spinach
1 firm pear
½ pink or red grapefruit, peeled
1 cup pineapple

Alternate ingredients, finishing with the pineapple or the grapefruit.

ASPARAGUS AND KALE SALAD

MAKES ABOUT 16 OUNCES

IMMUNE SUPPORT, DETOXIFYING, DIGESTION SUPPORT, MOOD LIFTER, STRUCTURE SUPPORT

8 asparagus spears
½ lemon
4 medium kale leaves
4 small carrots
8 small celery stalks
1 large cucumber

Alternate ingredients, finishing with the cucumber.

GARDEN STRAWBERRY WITH CARROT

MAKES ABOUT 16 OUNCES

IMMUNE SUPPORT, BRAIN HEALTH, DIGESTION SUPPORT, HEART HEALTH, MOOD LIFTER, STRUCTURE SUPPORT

1 large carrot
1 cup strawberries
8 medium romaine leaves
8 small celery stalks

Alternate ingredients, finishing with the celery.

BELL PEPPER AND BEETS WITH A KICK

MAKES ABOUT 16 OUNCES

IMMUNE SUPPORT, ANTI-INFLAMMATORY, DIGESTION SUPPORT, HEART HEALTH, MOOD LIFTER, STRUCTURE SUPPORT

1 medium golden or
   red beet
1 large yellow bell pepper
1-inch piece fresh
   ginger root
½ lemon
8 small celery stalks
½ large cucumber

Alternate ingredients, finishing with the cucumber.

ASPARAGUS, CHARD, AND BELL PEPPER BLEND

MAKES ABOUT 16 OUNCES

IMMUNE SUPPORT, BRAIN HEALTH, HEART HEALTH, MOOD LIFTER, STRUCTURE SUPPORT

8 asparagus spears
2 cups Swiss chard
½ lemon
1 orange, peeled
½ yellow bell pepper
1 large cucumber

Alternate ingredients, finishing with the cucumber.

HEALTHY CELLS

MAKES ABOUT 16 OUNCES

IMMUNE SUPPORT, DIGESTION SUPPORT, HEART HEALTH, STRUCTURE SUPPORT

4 large carrots
½ lemon
6 large celery stalks

Alternate ingredients, finishing with the celery.

ORANGE CHARD

MAKES ABOUT 16 OUNCES

IMMUNE SUPPORT, BRAIN HEALTH, DIGESTION SUPPORT, HEART HEALTH, MOOD LIFTER, STRUCTURE SUPPORT

8 small celery stalks
4 cups Swiss chard
2 oranges, peeled
½ large cucumber

Alternate ingredients, finishing with the cucumber.

CHARD, PEAR, AND CELERY HEALTH BOOST

MAKES ABOUT 16 OUNCES

IMMUNE SUPPORT, CLEANSING, DIGESTION SUPPORT, HEART HEALTH, MOOD LIFTER, STRUCTURE SUPPORT

4 small celery stalks
4 small Swiss chard leaves
1 firm pear
½ lemon
½ large cucumber

Alternate ingredients, finishing with the cucumber.

BEET, KALE, AND PEAR BOOST

MAKES ABOUT 16 OUNCES

IMMUNE SUPPORT, BRAIN HEALTH, CLEANSING, DETOXIFYING, DIGESTION SUPPORT, HEART HEALTH, MOOD LIFTER, STRUCTURE SUPPORT

1 medium golden or
   red beet
4 large kale leaves
½ yellow bell pepper
1 firm pear
½ large cucumber

Alternate ingredients, finishing with the cucumber.

MANGO, PEAR, AND BELL PEPPER QUENCHER

MAKES ABOUT 16 OUNCES

IMMUNE SUPPORT, CLEANSING, DIGESTION SUPPORT, MOOD LIFTER, STRUCTURE SUPPORT

½ yellow bell pepper
1 lime, peeled
1 cup mango
1 firm pear
8 small celery stalks

Alternate ingredients, finishing with the celery.

ORANGE CARROT

MAKES ABOUT 16 OUNCES

IMMUNE SUPPORT, DIGESTION SUPPORT, HEART HEALTH, MOOD LIFTER, STRUCTURE SUPPORT, WEIGHT LOSS

2 large carrots
2 cups spinach
4 large romaine leaves
2 oranges, peeled

Alternate ingredients, finishing with the orange.

ARUGULA AND ROOTS REFRESHER

MAKES ABOUT 16 OUNCES

IMMUNE SUPPORT, DETOXIFYING, DIGESTION SUPPORT, HEART HEALTH, MOOD LIFTER, STRUCTURE SUPPORT

Handful arugula
2 cups Swiss chard
8 parsley sprigs
1 lemon
1 medium beet
4 medium carrots
4 small celery stalks
1 orange, peeled

Alternate ingredients, finishing with the orange or the celery.

CARROT, ORANGE, AND SPROUTS SPLASH

MAKES ABOUT 16 OUNCES

IMMUNE SUPPORT, DETOXIFYING, HEART HEALTH, STRUCTURE SUPPORT

1 large carrot

1 cup sprouts (clover, broccoli, etc.)

½ lemon

2 oranges, peeled

½ large cucumber

Alternate ingredients, finishing with the cucumber.

PASSION MANGO

MAKES ABOUT 16 OUNCES

IMMUNE SUPPORT, BRAIN HEALTH, DIGESTION SUPPORT, HEART HEALTH, MOOD LIFTER, STRUCTURE SUPPORT

4 passion fruits

½ yellow bell pepper

1 cup mango

4 small celery stalks

1 large cucumber

Cut open the passion fruits and scoop out the flesh and seeds. Discard the rind. Alternate ingredients, finishing with the cucumber.

Ingredient Tip: Depending on where you live, passion fruit may be a higher-cost fruit that you splurge on occasionally. Shop for it in late summer into fall for the lowest prices.

SWEET PASSION PAPAYA

MAKES ABOUT 16 OUNCES

IMMUNE SUPPORT, DETOXIFYING, DIGESTION SUPPORT, STRUCTURE SUPPORT

2 passion fruits

1 cup black, purple, or red grapes

2 small limes, peeled

1 cup papaya

½ large cucumber

Cut open the passion fruits and scoop out the flesh and seeds. Discard the rind. Alternate ingredients, finishing with the cucumber.

PINEAPPLE PASSION

MAKES ABOUT 16 OUNCES

IMMUNE SUPPORT, ANTI-INFLAMMATORY, DIGESTION SUPPORT, STRUCTURE SUPPORT

2 passion fruits
1 cup pineapple
8 small celery stalks
½ large cucumber

Cut open the passion fruits and scoop out the flesh and seeds. Discard the rind. Alternate ingredients, finishing with the cucumber.

GARDEN SPROUTS

MAKES ABOUT 20 OUNCES

IMMUNE SUPPORT, BRAIN HEALTH, DETOXIFYING, DIGESTION SUPPORT, HEART HEALTH, MOOD LIFTER

1 orange, red, or yellow bell pepper

1 cup sprouts (clover, broccoli, etc.)

1 lime, peeled

1 small apple

8 small celery stalks

½ large cucumber

Alternate ingredients, finishing with the cucumber.

BLOOD ORANGE AND BEET TREAT

MAKES ABOUT 16 OUNCES

IMMUNE SUPPORT, ANTI-INFLAMMATORY, BRAIN HEALTH, HEART HEALTH, MOOD LIFTER, STRUCTURE SUPPORT

1 medium golden or red beet

1-inch piece fresh ginger root

4 small blood oranges or other oranges, peeled

1 large cucumber

Alternate ingredients, finishing with the cucumber.

Ingredient Tip: Blood oranges, also marketed as raspberry oranges, have three times the polyphenols and nine times the antioxidant capacity of navel oranges.

STAY STRONG

IMMUNE SUPPORT, BRAIN HEALTH, CLEANSING, DIGESTION SUPPORT, HEART HEALTH, MOOD LIFTER, STRUCTURE SUPPORT, WEIGHT LOSS

2 cups spinach
1 apple
1 firm pear
1 cup strawberries
4 small celery stalks

Alternate ingredients, finishing with the celery.

MINT-WATERMELON COOLER

MAKES ABOUT 16 OUNCES

IMMUNE SUPPORT, ANTI-INFLAMMATORY, BRAIN HEALTH, DIGESTION SUPPORT, HEART HEALTH, STRUCTURE SUPPORT

8 small celery stalks
20 fresh mint leaves
1 cup watermelon

Alternate ingredients, finishing with the watermelon.

SWEET POTATO ORANGE

MAKES ABOUT 16 OUNCES

IMMUNE SUPPORT, BRAIN HEALTH, DETOXIFYING, HEART HEALTH, MOOD LIFTER, STRUCTURE SUPPORT

2 large kale leaves
½ small sweet
  potato, peeled
2 large Swiss chard leaves
¼ lemon
1 orange, peeled
½ large cucumber

Alternate ingredients, finishing with the cucumber.

STRAWBERRY ROOTS

MAKES ABOUT 16 OUNCES

IMMUNE SUPPORT, ANTI-INFLAMMATORY, BRAIN HEALTH, DIGESTION SUPPORT, HEART HEALTH, STRUCTURE SUPPORT

4 large celery stalks

1 small sweet potato, peeled

1-inch piece fresh turmeric root

1 cup strawberries

2 oranges, peeled

1 large cucumber

Freshly ground black pepper (optional)

Alternate the produce, finishing with the cucumber. Stir the black pepper (if using) directly into the juice to increase your absorption of the curcumin in the turmeric.

PINEAPPLE AND CAMU CAMU

MAKES ABOUT 16 OUNCES

IMMUNE SUPPORT, ANTI-INFLAMMATORY, DIGESTION SUPPORT, HEART HEALTH, STRUCTURE SUPPORT

3 large carrots

1 orange, peeled

5 large celery stalks

1 cup pineapple

1 teaspoon camu camu powder

Alternate the produce, finishing with the pineapple or the celery. Stir the camu camu powder directly into the juice or place the juice and the camu camu powder in a jar and shake to combine.

Ingredient Tip: Camu camu fruit is a small, tart berry from the Amazon rain forest. Because it is so sour, it is normally consumed as a powder. One teaspoon of camu camu powder has 10 times the vitamin C of an orange. You can find it at most health food stores and online at NavitasOrganics.com and other online sellers.

CAMU GREENS

MAKES ABOUT 16 OUNCES

IMMUNE SUPPORT, BRAIN HEALTH, DETOXIFYING, HEART HEALTH, MOOD LIFTER, STRUCTURE SUPPORT, WEIGHT LOSS

4 medium Swiss
  chard leaves

½ small lemon

2 large bok choy stems

1 teaspoon camu
  camu powder

Alternate the produce, finishing with the bok choy. Stir the camu camu powder directly into the juice or place the juice and the camu camu powder in a jar and shake to combine.

FRUITY FENNEL

MAKES ABOUT 16 OUNCES

IMMUNE SUPPORT, BRAIN HEALTH, DIGESTION SUPPORT, HEART HEALTH, MOOD LIFTER, STRUCTURE SUPPORT, WEIGHT LOSS

1 small fennel bulb

2 cups spinach

½ cup blueberries

1 cup strawberries

1 apple

1 orange, peeled

Alternate ingredients, finishing with the orange.

ORANGE BELL BOOST

MAKES ABOUT 16 OUNCES

IMMUNE SUPPORT, HEART HEALTH, MOOD LIFTER

3 large carrots

½ orange bell pepper

2 Cara Cara or other
  small oranges, peeled

¼ lemon

1 large celery stalk

Juice the carrots, then alternate the remaining ingredients, finishing with the celery.

Pulp Tip: Reserve the carrot pulp and add ¼ to ½ cup of it to pancake batter.

TASTY BEET,
PAGE 156

CHAPTER 8

STRUCTURE SUPPORT

In this chapter, you will find mineral-rich juices designed to build strong bones and connective tissues, as well as healthy skin and blood. Dark leafy greens and broccoli are loaded with highly absorbable calcium. These vegetables provide other critical nutrients, including vitamin K and magnesium for bone strength. The fruits and vegetables high in vitamin C that are included in these recipes play an essential role in collagen production, important for healthy skin, ligaments, and tendons. The silica and magnesium in cucumbers are important components of collagen and all connective tissues.

Dark leafy greens are also rich in nonheme iron for healthy blood, which is made more absorbable in combination with fruits and vegetables high in vitamin C. Beets, carrots, celery, watercress, wheatgrass, and alfalfa grass are other foods with a long reputation as effective blood builders, supporting red blood cell production and healthy iron levels.

LIME, BLUEBERRY, AND BASIL BLEND

MAKES ABOUT 16 OUNCES

STRUCTURE SUPPORT, ANTI-INFLAMMATORY, BRAIN HEALTH, HEART HEALTH, MOOD LIFTER

4 large kale leaves
8 large basil leaves
1 cup blueberries
½ apple
1 small lime, peeled
1 cup watermelon

Alternate ingredients, finishing with the watermelon.

SUMMER BREEZE

MAKES ABOUT 20 OUNCES

STRUCTURE SUPPORT, ANTI-INFLAMMATORY, DIGESTION SUPPORT, HEART HEALTH

1 medium zucchini
1 lime, peeled
1 cup watermelon
½ cup fresh coconut water

Alternate the produce, finishing with the watermelon. Stir the coconut water directly into the juice.

Ingredient Tip: Look for seeded watermelons in late summer. Watermelon seeds contain magnesium, important for bone, heart, and immune health.

CARROT CRESS COCKTAIL

MAKES ABOUT 20 OUNCES

STRUCTURE SUPPORT, BRAIN HEALTH, CLEANSING, DETOXIFYING, HEART HEALTH, MOOD LIFTER

4 medium carrots
1 small zucchini
8 parsley sprigs
1 cup watercress
½ lemon
2 small apples

Alternate ingredients, finishing with the apple.

CHARD WITH GRAPEFRUIT, CARROT, AND PARSLEY

MAKES ABOUT 16 OUNCES

STRUCTURE SUPPORT, BRAIN HEALTH, HEART HEALTH, IMMUNE SUPPORT, MOOD LIFTER, WEIGHT LOSS

4 medium carrots

2 cups Swiss chard

10 parsley sprigs

1 large pink or red grapefruit, peeled

Alternate ingredients, finishing with the grapefruit.

SWEET STRENGTH

MAKES ABOUT 16 OUNCES

STRUCTURE SUPPORT, BRAIN HEALTH, DIGESTION SUPPORT, HEART HEALTH, MOOD LIFTER

2 large celery stalks

2 cups kale

2 cups Swiss Chard

2 small apples

1 large cucumber

Alternate ingredients, finishing with the cucumber.

BEET, APPLE, AND KALE COOLER

MAKES ABOUT 24 OUNCES

STRUCTURE SUPPORT, BRAIN HEALTH, DETOXIFYING, HEART HEALTH, MOOD LIFTER

1 medium golden or red beet

2 large kale leaves

5 parsley sprigs

1 apple

½ lemon

1 large cucumber

Alternate ingredients, finishing with the cucumber.

Ingredient Tip: You can reduce the amount of beet in your juice blend and slowly increase the amount as you build your palate for this blood-building root juice.

DELICIOUS BEET

MAKES ABOUT 16 OUNCES

STRUCTURE SUPPORT, BRAIN HEALTH, HEART HEALTH, IMMUNE SUPPORT, MOOD LIFTER

1 medium golden or red beet

1 large kale leaf

1 large celery stalk

2 small oranges, peeled

Alternate ingredients, finishing with the orange.

GARDEN BEET

MAKES ABOUT 16 OUNCES

STRUCTURE SUPPORT, BRAIN HEALTH, DIGESTION SUPPORT, HEART HEALTH, MOOD LIFTER

1 medium golden or red beet

1 orange, red, or yellow bell pepper

2-inch piece broccoli stem

2 large celery stalks

½ lemon

½ large cucumber

Alternate ingredients, finishing with the cucumber.

CITRUS, BOK CHOY, AND KALE COCKTAIL

MAKES ABOUT 20 OUNCES

STRUCTURE SUPPORT, BRAIN HEALTH, DETOXIFYING, HEART HEALTH, IMMUNE SUPPORT, MOOD LIFTER, WEIGHT LOSS

2 large bok choy stems

1 large kale leaf

½ large pink or red grapefruit, peeled

1 orange, peeled

1 large cucumber

Alternate ingredients, finishing with the cucumber.

Ingredient Tip: Most of the tissue-boosting silica in cucumbers is found in the peel, so buy organic cucumbers when possible and juice them with the peel.

DANDELION AND BOK CHOY DELIGHT

MAKES ABOUT 20 OUNCES

STRUCTURE SUPPORT, BRAIN HEALTH, DETOXIFYING, HEART HEALTH

2 medium bok
    choy stems

2 cups dandelion leaves

1 apple

1 large cucumber

Alternate ingredients, finishing with the cucumber.

Ingredient Tip: Cultivated dandelion greens can now be found at many grocery stores and health food stores. You can also forage for wild dandelion greens in pet-free areas where you are certain pesticides and chemical fertilizers have not been used.

FARMER'S MARKET

MAKES ABOUT 18 OUNCES

STRUCTURE SUPPORT, ANTI-INFLAMMATORY, BRAIN HEALTH, HEART HEALTH, DIGESTION SUPPORT, IMMUNE SUPPORT, MOOD LIFTER

2-inch piece
    broccoli stem

1-inch piece fresh
    turmeric root

10 large dandelion leaves

1 cup strawberries

3 large kale leaves

½ small fennel bulb

1 apple

1 orange, peeled

½ large cucumber

Freshly ground black
    pepper (optional)

Alternate the produce, finishing with the cucumber. Stir the black pepper (if using) directly into the juice to increase your absorption of the curcumin in the turmeric.

BEETROOT PARTY

MAKES ABOUT 16 OUNCES

STRUCTURE SUPPORT, BRAIN HEALTH, DETOXIFYING, HEART HEALTH, MOOD LIFTER

**1 medium golden or
red beet**

5 dandelion leaves

10 parsley sprigs

4 large carrots

1 small green apple

1 kiwifruit

1 medium cucumber

Alternate ingredients, finishing with the cucumber.

GINGERED CARROT

MAKES ABOUT 16 OUNCES

STRUCTURE SUPPORT, ANTI-INFLAMMATORY, DETOXIFYING, HEART HEALTH

1 pound carrots

**1-inch piece fresh
ginger root**

Handful parsley

¼ lemon

¼ lime, peeled

1 apple

Alternate ingredients, finishing with the apple.

Ingredient Tip: The beta-carotene in carrots protects against sunburn by increasing basal defense against UV light damage to skin. In one study, drinking 13½ ounces of carrot juice daily for 12 weeks led to a 45 percent reduction in sunburn.

FENNEL, CARROT, AND ORANGE BLEND

MAKES ABOUT 20 OUNCES

STRUCTURE SUPPORT, BRAIN HEALTH, DIGESTION SUPPORT, HEART HEALTH, IMMUNE SUPPORT

12 medium carrots

1 small fennel bulb

**1 Cara Cara or navel
orange, peeled**

Alternate ingredients, finishing with the orange.

DANDY CARROT CHARD

MAKES ABOUT 16 OUNCES

STRUCTURE SUPPORT, BRAIN HEALTH, DETOXIFYING, HEART HEALTH, MOOD LIFTER

12 small carrots
12 dandelion leaves
2 large Swiss chard leaves
1 lemon
1 large cucumber

Alternate ingredients, finishing with the cucumber.

BOK AROUND THE BLOCK

MAKES ABOUT 16 OUNCES

STRUCTURE SUPPORT, BRAIN HEALTH, DETOXIFYING, HEART HEALTH, MOOD LIFTER

2 large bok choy stems
10 sprigs parsley
1 large kale leaf
½ lemon
4 small carrots
1 cup tomato

Alternate ingredients, finishing with the tomato or the carrot.

Pulp Tip: Freeze all-vegetable juice pulp and vegetable scraps to make your own vegetable broth. Simply simmer 4 cups of water to every 1 to 2 cups of pulp/scraps along with some onion for 2 hours. Then, after cooking, use a fine mesh nut milk bag or cheesecloth to strain out the fiber for a silky smooth broth.

YUMMY GARDEN KALE

MAKES ABOUT 20 OUNCES

STRUCTURE SUPPORT, BRAIN HEALTH, DETOXIFYING, DIGESTION SUPPORT, HEART HEALTH, MOOD LIFTER

4 medium carrots
12 parsley sprigs
4 large kale leaves
1 kiwifruit
1 lemon
12 small celery stalks

Alternate ingredients, finishing with the celery.

TASTY BEET

MAKES ABOUT 16 OUNCES

STRUCTURE SUPPORT, BRAIN HEALTH, HEART HEALTH, IMMUNE SUPPORT

1 medium beet
4 medium carrots
12 small celery stalks
1 Cara Cara or navel
  orange, peeled

Alternate ingredients, finishing with the orange or the celery.

Ingredient Tip: Cara Cara oranges are a less acidic variety of navel oranges with a more complex flavor. They owe their rosy hue to the carotenoid lycopene, which can help protect against sunburn.

WATERMELON, CARROT, AND ROMAINE BLEND

MAKES ABOUT 28 OUNCES

STRUCTURE SUPPORT, ANTI-INFLAMMATORY, HEART HEALTH, MOOD LIFTER

4 medium carrots
12 medium
  romaine leaves
4 cups watermelon

Alternate ingredients, finishing with the watermelon.

PAPAYA, BEET, AND ORANGE BLEND

MAKES ABOUT 16 OUNCES

STRUCTURE SUPPORT, DIGESTION SUPPORT, HEART HEALTH, IMMUNE SUPPORT, MOOD LIFTER

1 medium beet
1 cup papaya
1 lime, peeled
1 Cara Cara or navel
  orange, peeled
1 large cucumber

Alternate ingredients, finishing with the cucumber.

TROPICAL BEET DANDY

MAKES ABOUT 16 OUNCES

STRUCTURE SUPPORT, ANTI-INFLAMMATORY, BRAIN HEALTH, HEART HEALTH, IMMUNE SUPPORT, MOOD LIFTER

1 medium golden or
  red beet

16 dandelion leaves

1 kiwifruit

½ orange, red, or yellow
  bell pepper

1 cup pineapple

Alternate ingredients, finishing with the pineapple.

SWEET STRAWBERRY ALFALFA

MAKES ABOUT 16 OUNCES

STRUCTURE SUPPORT, BRAIN HEALTH, HEART HEALTH, IMMUNE SUPPORT, MOOD LIFTER

½ cup alfalfa sprouts

2 large Swiss chard leaves

1 cup strawberries

2 kiwifruit

1 lime, peeled

1 orange, red, or yellow
  bell pepper

Alternate ingredients, finishing with the bell pepper.

SUMMER BEET

MAKES ABOUT 20 OUNCES

STRUCTURE SUPPORT, ANTI-INFLAMMATORY, BRAIN HEALTH, HEART HEALTH, MOOD LIFTER

1 medium golden or
  red beet

8 parsley sprigs

4 medium bok
  choy stems

2 cups watermelon

Alternate ingredients, finishing with
the watermelon.

FUN IN THE SUN

MAKES ABOUT 16 OUNCES

STRUCTURE SUPPORT, ANTI-INFLAMMATORY, BRAIN HEALTH, HEART HEALTH

¼ orange, red, or yellow
   bell pepper

2 medium bok
   choy stems

½ firm pear

½ cup strawberries

½ lemon

½ large cucumber

1 cup watermelon

Alternate ingredients, finishing with
the watermelon.

PINEAPPLE PLEASURES

MAKES ABOUT 20 OUNCES

STRUCTURE SUPPORT, ANTI-INFLAMMATORY, BRAIN HEALTH, CLEANSING, DIGESTION SUPPORT, HEART HEALTH, MOOD LIFTER

1 small fennel bulb

4 large kale leaves

1 firm pear

1 cup pineapple

1 large cucumber

Alternate ingredients, finishing with the cucumber.

ARUGULA, KIWI, AND PEAR PUNCH

MAKES ABOUT 16 OUNCES

STRUCTURE SUPPORT, BRAIN HEALTH, CLEANSING, DETOXIFYING, DIGESTION SUPPORT, HEART HEALTH, IMMUNE SUPPORT

1 cup arugula

2 kiwifruit

2 firm pears

½ large cucumber

Alternate ingredients, finishing with the cucumber.

DANDY APPLE PEAR

MAKES ABOUT 12 OUNCES

STRUCTURE SUPPORT, BRAIN HEALTH, CLEANSING, DETOXIFYING, DIGESTION SUPPORT, HEART HEALTH, MOOD LIFTER

8 dandelion leaves
1 large Swiss chard leaf
12 parsley sprigs
1 lime, peeled
1 firm pear
1 apple

Alternate ingredients, finishing with the apple.

BERRY GOOD GREENS

MAKES ABOUT 20 OUNCES

STRUCTURE SUPPORT, BRAIN HEALTH, DETOXIFYING, HEART HEALTH, IMMUNE SUPPORT, MOOD LIFTER

2-inch piece
  broccoli stem
1 large Swiss chard leaf
1 cup strawberries
1 lime, peeled
1 orange, peeled
1 apple

Alternate ingredients, finishing with the apple.

PINEAPPLE, MELON, AND CRUCIFEROUS GREENS

MAKES ABOUT 24 OUNCES

STRUCTURE SUPPORT, ANTI-INFLAMMATORY, BRAIN HEALTH, HEART HEALTH, IMMUNE SUPPORT, MOOD LIFTER

1 large orange, red, or
   yellow bell pepper

2-inch piece
   broccoli stem

4 medium kale leaves

½ lemon

8 small bok choy stems

1 cup pineapple

1 cup watermelon

Alternate ingredients, finishing with the watermelon.

GARDEN GLORY

MAKES ABOUT 16 OUNCES

STRUCTURE SUPPORT, BRAIN HEALTH, DETOXIFYING, DIGESTION SUPPORT, HEART HEALTH

2 large bok choy stems

6 dandelion leaves

½ cup tomato

1-inch piece broccoli stem

4 small celery stalks

¼ lemon

1 apple

Alternate ingredients, finishing with the apple.

WATERMELON AND GREENS DELIGHT

MAKES ABOUT 16 OUNCES

STRUCTURE SUPPORT, ANTI-INFLAMMATORY, BRAIN HEALTH, DETOXIFYING, HEART HEALTH,
IMMUNE SUPPORT, MOOD LIFTER

4 dandelion leaves
4 cups Swiss chard
½ lemon
1 orange, peeled
2 cups watermelon

Alternate ingredients, finishing with
the watermelon.

ORANGE GREENS REFRESHER

MAKES ABOUT 16 OUNCES

STRUCTURE SUPPORT, BRAIN HEALTH, DETOXIFYING, HEART HEALTH, IMMUNE SUPPORT,
MOOD LIFTER

1 large orange, red, or
yellow bell pepper
8 parsley sprigs
4 large romaine leaves
1 large kale leaf
2 small oranges, peeled
1 large cucumber

Alternate ingredients, finishing with the cucumber.

SIMPLY SWEET BEET

MAKES ABOUT 16 OUNCES

STRUCTURE SUPPORT, BRAIN HEALTH, HEART HEALTH, IMMUNE SUPPORT, MOOD LIFTER

1 medium golden or
red beet
1 large kale leaf
1 orange, peeled
1 cup raspberries
½ large cucumber

Alternate ingredients, finishing with the cucumber.

SUNNY KALE

MAKES ABOUT 16 OUNCES

STRUCTURE SUPPORT, ANTI-INFLAMMATORY, BRAIN HEALTH, DETOXIFYING, HEART HEALTH, IMMUNE SUPPORT, MOOD LIFTER, WEIGHT LOSS

3 large kale leaves
8 parsley sprigs
1 pink or red
  grapefruit, peeled
1 cup pineapple
1 apple

Alternate ingredients, finishing with the apple.

CHARMING CHARD

MAKES ABOUT 20 OUNCES

STRUCTURE SUPPORT, BRAIN HEALTH, HEART HEALTH, IMMUNE SUPPORT, MOOD LIFTER

1 large Swiss chard leaf
1 lime, peeled
1 cup mango
1 orange, peeled
1 large cucumber

Alternate ingredients, finishing with the cucumber.

GARDEN PEAR

MAKES ABOUT 16 OUNCES

STRUCTURE SUPPORT, BRAIN HEALTH, CLEANSING, DETOXIFYING, DIGESTION SUPPORT, HEART HEALTH, IMMUNE SUPPORT, MOOD LIFTER

1 medium golden or
  red beet
2 large kale leaves
½ cup cauliflower
1 firm pear
4 large celery stalks

Alternate ingredients, finishing with the celery.

BERRY GOOD KALE

MAKES ABOUT 16 OUNCES

STRUCTURE SUPPORT, BRAIN HEALTH, CLEANSING, DIGESTION SUPPORT, HEART HEALTH, IMMUNE SUPPORT, MOOD LIFTER

3 large kale leaves
1 cup raspberries
1 firm pear
2 oranges, peeled

Alternate ingredients, finishing with the orange.

BEET AND BLACKBERRY WITH GREENS

MAKES ABOUT 16 OUNCES

STRUCTURE SUPPORT, BRAIN HEALTH, DETOXIFYING, HEART HEALTH, IMMUNE SUPPORT, MOOD LIFTER

1 cup blackberries
1 medium golden or
  red beet
1 large kale leaf
2 large romaine leaves
2 large bok choy stems
1 orange, red, or yellow
  bell pepper
½ large cucumber

Alternate ingredients, finishing with the cucumber.

LEMONY CARROT AND KALE COOLER

MAKES ABOUT 16 OUNCES

STRUCTURE SUPPORT, BRAIN HEALTH, HEART HEALTH, IMMUNE SUPPORT, MOOD LIFTER

1 large carrot
2 large kale leaves
1 lemon
2 oranges, peeled
½ large cucumber

Alternate ingredients, finishing with the cucumber.

GREEN GOODNESS

MAKES ABOUT 16 OUNCES

STRUCTURE SUPPORT, BRAIN HEALTH, DETOXIFYING, HEART HEALTH, MOOD LIFTER

3 large kale leaves
8 parsley sprigs
1 lime, peeled
2 large Swiss chard leaves
½ large cucumber

Alternate ingredients, finishing with the cucumber.

BLUEBERRY-BASIL GREENS

MAKES ABOUT 16 OUNCES

STRUCTURE SUPPORT, BRAIN HEALTH, DIGESTION SUPPORT, HEART HEALTH, MOOD LIFTER

1 cup blueberries
8 large basil leaves
1 large kale leaf
½ lemon
2 Swiss chard leaves
2 large celery stalks

Alternate ingredients, finishing with the celery.

ORANGE CHARD COOLER

MAKES ABOUT 16 OUNCES

STRUCTURE SUPPORT, DIGESTION SUPPORT, HEART HEALTH, IMMUNE SUPPORT, MOOD LIFTER

4 large celery stalks
1 large Swiss chard leaf
2 oranges, peeled
¼ lemon
½ large cucumber

Alternate ingredients, finishing with the cucumber.

ASPARAGUS, KIWI, AND APPLE BLEND

MAKES ABOUT 16 OUNCES

STRUCTURE SUPPORT, BRAIN HEALTH, DETOXIFYING, HEART HEALTH, IMMUNE SUPPORT, MOOD LIFTER

12 medium
  asparagus spears
2-inch piece
  broccoli stem
1 kiwifruit
½ lemon
1 apple

Alternate ingredients, finishing with the apple.

BEET, CARROT, AND WATERCRESS QUENCHER

MAKES ABOUT 16 OUNCES

STRUCTURE SUPPORT, BRAIN HEALTH, DETOXIFYING, HEART HEALTH, MOOD LIFTER

½ medium beet
3 large carrots
4 cilantro sprigs
1 cup watercress
Handful spinach
1 small lemon
1 apple

Alternate ingredients, finishing with the apple.

WATERMELON LIMEADE

MAKES ABOUT 20 OUNCES

STRUCTURE SUPPORT, ANTI-INFLAMMATORY, HEART HEALTH

2 limes, peeled
4 cups watermelon

Alternate ingredients, finishing with the watermelon.

STRAWBERRY GREENS

MAKES ABOUT 20 OUNCES

STRUCTURE SUPPORT, BRAIN HEALTH, DETOXIFYING, DIGESTION SUPPORT, HEART HEALTH, IMMUNE SUPPORT, MOOD LIFTER

4 small bok choy stems
4 medium romaine leaves
12 sprigs parsley
½ cup alfalfa sprouts
1 cup strawberries
1 lemon
12 small celery stalks
1 orange, peeled

Alternate ingredients, finishing with the orange or the celery.

ARUGULA, MANGO, AND CELERY BLEND

MAKES ABOUT 16 OUNCES

STRUCTURE SUPPORT, DETOXIFYING, DIGESTION SUPPORT, IMMUNE SUPPORT

Handful arugula
1 cup mango
3 large celery stalks
1 apple

Alternate ingredients, finishing with the apple or the celery.

TART AND TASTY

MAKES ABOUT 16 OUNCES

STRUCTURE SUPPORT, BRAIN HEALTH, DIGESTION SUPPORT, HEART HEALTH

Handful arugula
3 large celery stalks
½ lemon
1 green apple

Alternate ingredients, finishing with the apple.

MINTED WATERMELON AND ARUGULA REFRESHER

MAKES ABOUT 20 OUNCES

STRUCTURE SUPPORT, ANTI-INFLAMMATORY, DETOXIFYING, HEART HEALTH

½ cup arugula
½ lemon
8 medium fresh
   mint leaves
1 apple
2 cups watermelon

Alternate ingredients, finishing with the watermelon.

FENNEL-KIWI COOLER

MAKES ABOUT 20 OUNCES

STRUCTURE SUPPORT, DETOXIFYING, DIGESTION SUPPORT, IMMUNE SUPPORT

1 small fennel bulb
1 kiwifruit
1 cup strawberries
8 parsley sprigs
1 medium cucumber

Alternate ingredients, finishing with the cucumber.

STRAWBERRY, GRAPEFRUIT, AND CHARD

MAKES ABOUT 16 OUNCES

STRUCTURE SUPPORT, BRAIN HEALTH, HEART HEALTH, IMMUNE SUPPORT, MOOD LIFTER, WEIGHT LOSS

4 medium Swiss
   chard leaves
½ pink or red
   grapefruit, peeled
1 cup strawberries
1 large cucumber

Alternate ingredients, finishing with the cucumber.

CELERY, KIWI,
AND KALE BLEND,
PAGE 169

ORANGE, GRAPEFRUIT, AND GREENS

MAKES ABOUT 16 OUNCES

STRUCTURE SUPPORT, BRAIN HEALTH, HEART HEALTH, IMMUNE SUPPORT, MOOD LIFTER, WEIGHT LOSS

8 dandelion leaves

4 medium Swiss chard leaves

½ pink or red grapefruit, peeled

2 blood oranges or other small oranges, peeled

Alternate ingredients, finishing with the orange.

Ingredient Tip: The beautiful crimson color of blood oranges is due to their high levels of anthocyanins, antioxidants that fight free radicals that promote disease and early aging of the skin. The vitamin C and other antioxidants found in citrus fruits may be beneficial for the skin when consumed as food or juice and metabolized by the body.

CELERY, KIWI, AND KALE BLEND

MAKES ABOUT 16 OUNCES

STRUCTURE SUPPORT, BRAIN HEALTH, DIGESTION SUPPORT, HEART HEALTH, IMMUNE SUPPORT, MOOD LIFTER

4 medium kale leaves

4 kiwifruit

12 small celery stalks

Alternate ingredients, finishing with the celery.

CHARD-KIWI COOLER

MAKES ABOUT 16 OUNCES

STRUCTURE SUPPORT, BRAIN HEALTH, HEART HEALTH, IMMUNE SUPPORT, MOOD LIFTER

4 large Swiss chard leaves

2 kiwifruit

1 large cucumber

Alternate ingredients, finishing with the cucumber.

GREEN GREATNESS

MAKES ABOUT 16 OUNCES

STRUCTURE SUPPORT, BRAIN HEALTH, DETOXIFYING, DIGESTION SUPPORT, HEART HEALTH, IMMUNE SUPPORT, MOOD LIFTER

6 small celery stalks
2 large Swiss chard leaves
2 medium kale leaves
2 kiwifruit
1 small lemon
½ large cucumber

Alternate ingredients, finishing with the cucumber.

BLUEBERRY AND ARUGULA SALAD

MAKES ABOUT 20 OUNCES

STRUCTURE SUPPORT, BRAIN HEALTH, HEART HEALTH, IMMUNE SUPPORT, MOOD LIFTER

1 cup blueberries
½ cup arugula
8 cilantro sprigs
8 small celery stalks
1 large cucumber

Alternate ingredients, finishing with the cucumber.

BLACKBERRY, KALE, AND ORANGE BLEND

MAKES ABOUT 20 OUNCES

STRUCTURE SUPPORT, BRAIN HEALTH, HEART HEALTH, IMMUNE SUPPORT

1 cup blackberries
4 medium kale leaves
2 large romaine leaves
2 blood oranges, peeled
½ large cucumber

Alternate ingredients, finishing with the cucumber.

MORNING GLORY

MAKES ABOUT 16 OUNCES

STRUCTURE SUPPORT, BRAIN HEALTH, HEART HEALTH

1 small golden beet
½ yellow bell pepper
**2 blood oranges or other
    small oranges, peeled**
¼ lemon
8 medium carrots

Alternate ingredients, finishing with the carrot.

TROPICAL BERRY-KALE BLEND

MAKES ABOUT 16 OUNCES

**STRUCTURE SUPPORT, ANTI-INFLAMMATORY, BRAIN HEALTH, DIGESTION SUPPORT,
IMMUNE SUPPORT**

2 cups pineapple
1½ cups strawberries
3 large kale leaves
5 parsley sprigs
½ cucumber

Juice the pineapple and the strawberries first.
Alternate the remaining ingredients, finishing with
the cucumber.

Pulp Tip: Reserve the pineapple and strawberry pulp and use it
as a fruit spread on toast or add it to a smoothie.

PINEAPPLE JOY

MAKES ABOUT 20 OUNCES

**STRUCTURE SUPPORT, ANTI-INFLAMMATORY, BRAIN HEALTH, CLEANSING, DIGESTION SUPPORT,
HEART HEALTH, MOOD LIFTER**

**1 orange, red, or yellow
    bell pepper**
4 medium kale leaves
1 firm pear
2 cups pineapple

Alternate ingredients, finishing with the pineapple.

PINEAPPLE KICKS,
PAGE 35

RESOURCES

WEBSITES

Drugs.com/drug_interactions.html

Drug interactions checker

Friedas.com/Where-To-Buy

Locate stores near you that sell Stokes Purple sweet potatoes

HealthforceSuperfoods.com

Online retailer where you can purchase Vitamineral Green

JuiceCertification.com

Become a certified juice therapist trained in the Juice Guru Method

NavitasOrganics.com

Online retailer that offers organic products for a plant-based diet

NutritionFacts.org

Short videos and articles that explain the latest studies, making nutrition science easier to understand and implement

Sproutman.com

Online retailer where you can purchase Sproutman Organic Freeze-Dried Wheatgrass Juice Powder

StephanieLeach.com

Articles, recipes, and free resources on juicing and having a whole food, plant-based lifestyle, along with information on private and group health-coaching programs and juice cleanses

YouTube.com/c/StephanieLeach

Videos on juicing and creating a plant-based lifestyle for a strong, healthy body

BOOKS

The China Study: The Most Comprehensive Study of Nutrition Ever Conducted, revised and expanded edition, by T. Colin Campbell, PhD, and Thomas M. Campbell II, MD

The Complete Idiot's Guide to Juice Fasting by Steven Prussack and Bo Rinaldi

The Detox Miracle Sourcebook by Robert Morse, ND

Eat for Life: The Breakthrough Nutrient-Rich Program for Longevity, Disease Reversal, and Sustained Weight Loss by Joel Fuhrman, MD

Fresh Vegetable and Fruit Juices by N. W. Walker

Juice Guru: Transform Your Life by Adding One Juice a Day by Steve Prussack and Julie Prussack

The Ultimate Book of Modern Juicing by Mimi Kirk

REFERENCES

Aga, Miho, Kanso Iwaki, Yasuto Ueda, Shimpei Ushio, Naoya Masaki, Shigeharu Fukuda, Tetsuo Kimoto, Masao Ikeda, and Masashi Kurimoto. "Preventive Effect of *Coriandrum sativum* (Chinese Parsley) on Localized Lead Deposition in ICR Mice." *Journal of Ethnopharmacology* 77, no. 2–3 (October 2001): 203–8. doi.org/10.1016/s0378-8741(01)00299-9.

Agarwal, Rakhi, Sudhir K. Goel, and Jai Raj Behari. "Detoxification and Antioxidant Effects of Curcumin in Rats Experimentally Exposed to Mercury." *Journal of Applied Toxicology* 30, no. 5 (July 2010): 457–68. doi.org/10.1002/jat.1517.

Anand, Preetha, Chitra Sundaram, Sonia Jhurani, Ajaikumar B. Kunnumakkara, and Bharat B. Aggarwal. "Curcumin and Cancer: An 'Old-Age' Disease with an 'Age-Old' Solution." *Cancer Letters* 267, no. 1 (August 18, 2008): 133–64. doi.org/10.1016/j.canlet.2008.03.025.

Aptekmann, Nancy Preising, and Thais Borges Cesar. "Orange Juice Improved Lipid Profile and Blood Lactate of Overweight Middle-Aged Women Subjected to Aerobic Training." *Maturitas* 67, no. 4 (December 2010): 343–47. doi.org/10.1016/j.maturitas.2010.07.009.

Aune, Dagfinn, Edward Giovannucci, Paolo Boffetta, Lars T. Fadnes, NaNa Keum, Teresa Norat, Darren C. Greenwood, Elio Riboli, Lars J. Vatten, and Serena Tonstad. "Fruit and Vegetable Intake and the Risk of Cardiovascular Disease, Total Cancer and All-Cause Mortality—A Systematic Review and Dose-Response Meta-Analysis of Prospective Studies." *International Journal of Epidemiology* 46, no. 3 (June 2017): 1029–56. doi.org/10.1093/ije/dyw319.

Bauer, Brent A. "Can Vitamin C Improve Your Mood?" Mayo Clinic. August 30, 2017. mayoclinic.org/healthy-lifestyle/nutrition-and-healthy-eating /expert-answers/benefits-vitamin-c/faq-20058271.

Belviranli, Muaz, Nilsel Okudan, Kismet Esra Nurullahoğlu Atalik, and Mehmet Öz. "Curcumin Improves Spatial Memory and Decreases Oxidative Damage in Aged Female Rats." *Biogerontology* 14, no. 2 (2013): 187–96. doi.org/10.1007/s10522-013-9422-y.

Ben-Ayre, E., E. Goldin, D. Wengrower, A. Stamper, R. Kohn, and E. Berry. "Wheat Grass Juice in the Treatment of Active Distal Ulcerative Colitis: A Randomized Double-Blind Placebo-Controlled Trial." *Scandinavian Journal of Gastroenterology* 37, no. 4 (2002): 444–49. doi.org/10.1080/003655202317316088.

Bolzetta, Francesco, Nicola Veronese, Brendon Stubbs, Marianna Noale, Alberto Vaona, Jacopo Demurtas, Stefano Celotto, et al. "The Relationship between Dietary Vitamin K and Depressive Symptoms in Late Adulthood: A Cross-Sectional Analysis from a Large Cohort Study." *Nutrients* 11, no. 4: 787. doi.org/10.3390/nu11040787.

Chainani-Wu, Nita. "Safety and Anti-Inflammatory Activity of Curcumin: A Component of Turmeric (*Curcuma longa*)." *Journal of Alternative and Complementary Medicine* 9, no. 1 (February 2003): 161–68. doi.org/10.1089/107555303321223035.

Clifford, Tom, Glyn Howatson, Daniel J. West, and Emma J. Stevenson. "The Potential Benefits of Red Beetroot Supplementation in Health and Disease." *Nutrients* 7, no. 4 (April 2015): 2801–22. doi.org/10.3390/nu7042801.

Coelho, Raquel Cristina Lopes Assis, Helen Hermana M. Hermsdorff, and Josefina Bressan. "Anti-Inflammatory Properties of Orange Juice: Possible Favorable Molecular and Metabolic Effects." *Plant Foods for Human Nutrition* 68 (2013): 1–10. doi.org/10.1007/s11130-013-0343-3.

Dai, Qi, Amy R. Borenstein, Yougui Wu, James C. Jackson, and Eric B. Larson. "Fruit and Vegetable Juices and Alzheimer's Disease: The *Kame* Project." *The American Journal of Medicine* 119, no. 9 (September 2006): 751–59. doi.org/10.1016/j.amjmed.2006.03.045.

Devore, Elizabeth E., Jae Hee Kang, Monique Breteler, and Francine Grodstein. "Dietary Intakes of Berries and Flavonoids in Relation to

Cognitive Decline." *Annuals of Neurology* 72, no. 1 (July 2012): 135–43. doi.org/10.1002/ana.23594.

Drugs.com. "Drugs Interactions Checker." drugs.com/drug_interactions.html.

Farzaei, Mohammad Hosein, Mahdi Zobeiri, Fatemeh Parvizi, Fardous F. El-Senduny, Ilias Marmouzi, Ericsson Coy-Barrera, Rozita Naseri, Seyed Mohammad Nabavi, Roja Rahimi, and Mohammad Abdollahi. "Curcumin in Liver Diseases: A Systematic Review of the Cellular Mechanisms of Oxidative Stress and Clinical Perspective." *Nutrients* 10, no. 7 (July 2018): 855. doi.org/10.3390/nu10070855.

Figueroa, Arturo, Marcos A. Sanchez-Gonzalez, Alexei Wong, and Bahram H. Arjmandi. "Watermelon Extract Supplementation Reduces Ankle Blood Pressure and Carotid Augmentation Index in Obese Adults with Prehypertension or Hypertension." *American Journal of Hypertension* 25, no. 6 (June 2012): 640–43. doi.org/10.1038/ajh.2012.20.

Freedman, Neal D., Yikyung Park, Amy F. Subar, Albert R. Hollenbeck, Michael F. Leitzmann, Arthur Schatzkin, and Christian C. Abnet. "Fruit and Vegetable Intake and Esophageal Cancer in a Large Perspective Cohort Study." *International Journal of Cancer* 121, no. 12 (December 2007): 2753–60. doi.org/10.1002/ijc.22993.

Greger, Michael. *How Not to Diet: The Groundbreaking Science of Healthy, Permanent Weight Loss.* New York: Flatiron Books, 2019.

Griep, Linda M. Oude, W. M. Monique Verschuren, Daan Kromhout, Marga C. Ocké, and Johanna M. Geleijnse. "Colours of Fruit and Vegetables and 10-Year Incidence of CHD." *British Journal of Nutrition* 106, no. 10 (November 2011): 1562–69. doi.org/10.1017/S0007114511001942.

Gul, Zeynep, and Manoj Monga. "Medical and Dietary Therapy for Kidney Stone Prevention." *Korean Journal of Urology* 55, no. 12 (December 2014): 775–79. doi.org/10.4111/kju.2014.55.12.775.

Han, Jeong-Swa, Hye-Jin Lee, Tae-Seok Kim, and Myung-Hee Kang. "The Effect of *Glutathione S-Transferase M1* and *T1* Polymorphisms on Blood Pressure, Blood Glucose, and Lipid Profiles Following the Supplementation of Kale (*Brassica oleracea acephala*) Juice in South Korean Subclinical

Hypertensive Patients." *Nutrition Research and Practice* 9, no. 1 (February 2015): 49–56. doi.org/10.4162/nrp.2015.9.1.49.

Hodges, Romilly E., and Deanna M. Minich. "Modulation of Metabolic Detoxification Pathways Using Foods and Food-Derived Components: A Scientific Review with Clinical Application." *Journal of Nutrition and Metabolism* (2015). doi.org/10.1155/2015/760689.

Huang, Guan-Jhong, Ming-Jyh Sheu, Hsien-Jung Chen, Yuan-Shiun Chang, and Yaw-Huei Lin. "Growth Inhibition and Induction of Apoptosis in NB4 Promyelocytic Leukemia Cells by Trypsin Inhibitor from Sweet Potato Storage Roots." *Journal of Agricultural and Food Chemistry* 55, no. 7 (April 2007): 2548–53. doi.org/10.1021/jf063008m.

Humanitas Research Hospital. "Skin: Blood Oranges Used to Treat Erythema and Free Radicals?" October 12, 2017. humanitas.net/news/skin-blood-oranges-used-to-treat-erythema-and-free-radicals.

Hyson, Dianne, Deborah Studebaker-Hallman, Paul A. Davis, and M. Eric Gershwin. "Apple Juice Consumption Reduces Plasma Low-Density Lipoprotein Oxidation in Healthy Men and Women." *Journal of Medicinal Food* 3, no. 4 (January 2000): 159–66. doi.org/10.1089/jmf.2000.3.159.

Imran, Muhammad, Muhammad Sajid Arshad, Masood Sadiq Butt, Joong-Ho Kwon, Muhammad Umair Arshad, and Muhammad Tauseef Sultan. "Mangiferin: A Natural Miracle Bioactive Compound against Lifestyle Related Disorders." *Lipids in Health and Disease* 16 (2017). doi.org/10.1186/s12944-017-0449-y.

Jedrychowski, Wieslaw, and Umberto Maugeri. "An Apple a Day May Hold Colorectal Cancer at Bay: Recent Evidence from a Case-Control Study." *Reviews on Environmental Health* 24, no. 1 (January–March 2009): 59–74. doi.org/10.1515/reveh.2009.24.1.59.

Johnson, Sarah A., and Bahram H. Arjmandi. "Evidence for Anti-cancer Properties of Blueberries: A Mini-Review." *Anti-cancer Agents in Medicinal Chemistry* 13, no. 8 (2013): 1142–48. doi.org/10.2174/18715206113139990137.

Johnston, Carol S., Samantha Quagliano, and Serena White. "Vinegar Ingestion at Mealtime Reduced Fasting Blood Glucose Concentrations in Healthy Adults at Risk for Type 2 Diabetes." *Journal of Functional Foods* 5, no. 4 (October 2013): 2007–11. doi.org/10.1016/j.jff.2013.08.003.

Johnston, Kelly L., Michael N. Clifford, and Linda M. Morgan. "Possible Role for Apple Juice Phenolic Compounds in the Acute Modification of Glucose Tolerance and Gastrointestinal Hormone Secretion in Humans." *Journal of the Science of Food and Agriculture* 82, no. 15 (December 2002): 1800–5. doi.org/10.1002/jsfa.1264.

Kemble, Joe. "Should I Wash Fresh Fruit in Vinegar?" Best Food Facts. September 26, 2018. bestfoodfacts.org/fruit-vinegar.

Kent, Christopher. "Glaucoma Risk: The Nutrition Connection." *Review of Ophthalmology*. November 20, 2008. reviewofophthalmology.com/article /glaucoma-risk-the-nutrition-connection.

Kim, Soo Yeon, Sun Yoon, Soo Mi Kwon, Kye Sook Park, and Yang Cha Lee-Kim. "Kale Juice Improves Coronary Artery Disease Risk Factors in Hypercholesterolemic Men." *Biomedical and Environmental Sciences* 21, no. 2 (February 2008): 91–97. doi.org/10.1016/S0895-3988(08)60012-4.

Kowalska, Katarzyna, Anna Olejnik, Joanna Rychlik, and Włodzimierz Grajek. "Cranberries (*Oxycoccus quadripetalus*) Inhibit Lipid Metabolism and Modulate Leptin and Adiponectin Secretion in 3T3-L1 Adipocytes." *Food Chemistry* 185 (October 2015): 383–88. doi.org/10.1016/j .foodchem.2015.03.152.

Lefort, Émilie C., and Jonathan Blay. "Apigenin and Its Impact on Gastrointestinal Cancers." *Molecular Nutrition & Food Research* 57, no. 1 (January 2013): 126–44. doi.org/10.1002/mnfr.201200424.

Li, Peng-Gao, Tai-Hua Mu, and Le Deng. "Anticancer Effects of Sweet Potato Protein on Human Colorectal Cancer Cells." *World Journal of Gastroenterology* 19, no. 21 (June 2013): 3300–8. doi.org/10.3748/wjg.v19.i21.3300.

Linseisen, Jakob, Sabine Rohrmann, Anthony Miller, H. Bas Bueno-de-Mesquita, Frederike Büchner, Paolo Vineis, Antonio Agudo, et al. "Fruit and

Vegetable Consumption and Lung Cancer Risk: Updated Information from the European Prospective Investigation into Cancer and Nutrition (EPIC)." *International Journal of Cancer* 121, no. 5 (September 2007): 1103–14. doi.org/10.1002/ijc.22807.

Linus Pauling Institute. "Chlorophyll and Chlorophyllin." Oregon State University. lpi.oregonstate.edu/mic/dietary-factors/phytochemicals/chlorophyll-chlorophyllin.

Mahesh, Malleswarapu, Munuglala Bharathi, Mooli Raja Gopal Reddy, Manchiryala Sravan Kumar, Uday Kumar Putcha, Ayyalasomayajula Vajreswari, and Shanmugam Jeyakumar. "Carrot Juice Administration Decreases Liver Stearoyl-CoA Desaturase 1 and Improves Docosahexaenoic Acid Levels, but Not Steatosis in High Fructose Diet-Fed Weanling Wistar Rats." *Preventive Nutrition and Food Science* 21, no. 3 (September 2016): 171–80. doi.org/10.3746/pnf.2016.21.3.171.

Miller, Marshall G., and Barbara Shukitt-Hale. "Berry Fruit Enhances Beneficial Signaling in the Brain." *Journal of Agricultural and Food Chemistry* 60, no. 23 (2012): 5709–15. doi.org/10.1021/jf2036033.

Morand, Christine, Claude Dubray, Dragan Milenkovic, Delphine Lioger, Jean François Martin, Augustin Scalbert, and Andrzej Mazur. "Hesperidin Contributes to the Vascular Protective Effects of Orange Juice: A Randomized Crossover Study in Healthy Volunteers." *American Journal of Clinical Nutrition* 93, no. 1 (January 2011): 73–80. doi.org/10.3945/ajcn.110.004945.

Munday, Rex, Yuesheng Zhang, Christine M. Munday, Meghana V. Bapardekar, and Joseph D. Paonessa. "Structure-Activity Relationships and Organ Specificity in the Induction of GST and NQO1 by Alkyl-Aryl Isothiocyanates." *Pharmaceutical Research* 25, no. 9 (September 2008): 2164–70. doi.org/10.1007/s11095-008-9595-2.

Murphy, Mary M., Erin C. Barrett, Kara A. Bresnahan, and Leila M. Barraj. "100% Fruit Juice and Measures of Glucose Control and Insulin Sensitivity: A Systematic Review and Meta-Analysis of Randomised Controlled Trials." *Journal of Nutritional Science* 6 (December 15, 2017): e59. doi.org/10.1017/jns.2017.63.

National Institute of Diabetes and Digestive and Kidney Diseases. "Digestive Diseases Statistics for the United States." US Department of Health and Human Services, November 2014. niddk.nih.gov/health-information /health-statistics/digestive-diseases.

Niederberger, Katherine E., David R. Tennant, and Phillip Bellion. "Dietary Intake of Phloridzin from Natural Occurrence in Foods." *British Journal of Nutrition* 123, no. 8 (April 28, 2020): 942–50. doi.org/10.1017 /S0007114520000033.

Novotny, Janet A., David J. Baer, Christina Khoo, Sarah K. Gebauer, and Craig S. Charron. "Cranberry Juice Consumption Lowers Markers of Cardiometabolic Risk, Including Blood Pressure and Circulating C-Reactive Protein, Triglyceride, and Glucose Concentrations in Adults." *The Journal of Nutrition* 145, no. 6 (June 2015): 1185–93. doi.org/10.3945/jn.114.203190.

Odvina, Clarita V. "Comparative Value of Orange Juice versus Lemonade in Reducing Stone-Forming Risk." *Clinical Journal of the American Society of Nephrology* 1, no. 6 (November 2006): 1269–74. doi.org/10.2215 /CJN.00800306.

Pandurangan, Ashok Kumar, and Norhaizan Mohd Esa. "Luteolin, a Bioflavonoid Inhibits Colorectal Cancer through Modulation of Multiple Signaling Pathways: A Review." *Asian Pacific Journal of Cancer Prevention* 15, no. 14 (2014): 5501–8. doi.org/10.7314/APJCP.2014.15.14.5501.

Paquette, Martine, Ana S. Medina Larqué, S. J. Weisnagel, Yves Desjardins, Julie Marois, Geneviève Pilon, Stéphanie Dudonné, André Marette, and Hélène Jacques. "Strawberry and Cranberry Polyphenols Improve Insulin Sensitivity in Insulin-Resistant, Non-Diabetic Adults: A Parallel, Double-Blind, Controlled and Randomised Clinical Trial." *British Journal of Nutrition* 117, no. 4 (February 28, 2017): 519–31. doi.org/10.1017/S0007114517000393.

Polizzi, Stephanie. "Say NO to Disease." OSU Extension Family & Community Health. June 2013. extension.oregonstate.edu/sites/default/files/documents /8836/asay-no-disease-handout.pdf.

Prasad, Sahdeo, and Amit K. Tyagi. "Ginger and Its Constituents: Role in Prevention and Treatment of Gastrointestinal Cancer." *Gastroenterology Research and Practice* (2015). doi.org/10.1155/2015/142979.

Presley, Tennille D., Ashley R. Morgan, Erika Bechtold, William Clodfelter, Robin W. Dove, Janine M. Jennings, Robert A. Kraft, et al. "Acute Effect of a High Nitrate Diet on Brain Perfusion in Older Adults." *Nitric Oxide* 24, no. 1 (January 2011): 34–42. doi.org/10.1016/j.niox.2010.10.002.

Rathnavelu, Vidhya, Noorjahan Banu Alitheen, Subramaniam Sohila, Samikannu Kanagesan, and Rajendran Ramesh. "Potential Role of Bromelian in Clinical and Therapeutic Applications." *Biomedical Reports* 5, no. 3 (September 2016): 283–88. doi.org/10.3892/br.2016.720.

Reiland, Holly, and Joanne Slavin. "Systematic Review of Pears and Health." *Nutrition Today* 50, no. 6 (November 2015): 301–5. doi.org/10.1097/NT.0000000000000112.

Ren, Si-chong, Qi-feng Suo, Wen-ting Du, Hong Pan, Ming-ming Yang, Ruo-han Wang, and Ji Liu. "Quercetin Permeability across Blood-Brain Barrier and Its Effect on the Viability of U251 Cells." *Sichuan Da Xue Xue Bao Yi Xue Ban* 41, no.5 (September 2010): 751–54, 759. pubmed.ncbi.nlm.nih.gov/21302433.

Rhode, Jennifer, Sarah Fogoros, Suzanna Zick, Heather Wahl, Kent A. Griffith, Jennifer Huang, and J. Rebecca Liu. "Ginger Inhibits Cell Growth and Modulates Angiogenic Factors in Ovarian Cancer Cells." *BMC Complementary and Alternative Medicine* 7 (2007): 44. doi.org/10.1186/1472-6882-7-44.

Sahebkar, Amirhossein, Claudio Ferri, Paolo Giorgini, Simona Bo, Petr Nachtigal, and Davide Grassi. "Effects of Pomegranate Juice on Blood Pressure: A Systematic Review and Meta-Analysis of Randomized Controlled Trials." *Pharmacological Research* 115 (January 2017): 149–61. doi.org/10.1016/j.phrs.2016.11.018.

Sandhya, V. G., and T. Rajamohan. "Comparative Evaluation of the Hypolipidemic Effects of Coconut Water and Lovastatin in Rats Fed Fat-Cholesterol Enriched Diet." *Food and Chemical Toxicology* 46, no. 12 (December 2008): 3586–92. doi.org/10.1016/j.fct.2008.08.030.

Souquet, J. M., B. Labarbe, C. Le Guernevé, V. Cheynier, and M. Moutounet. "Phenolic Composition of Grape Stems." *Journal of Agricultural and Food Chemistry* 48, no. 4 (April 2000): 1076–80. doi.org/10.1021/jf991171u.

Stahl, Wilhelm, Ulrike Heinrich, Olivier Aust, Hagen Tronnier, and Helmut Sies. "Lycopene-Rich Products and Dietary Photoprotection." *Photochemical & Photobiological Sciences* 5 (2006): 238–42. doi.org/10.1039/b505312a.

Stein, Traci. "Depression Won't Go Away? Folate Could Be the Answer." *Psychology Today.* October 6, 2013. psychologytoday.com/us/blog/the -integrationist/201310/depression-wont-go-away-folate-could -be-the-answer.

Usharani, P., A. A. Mateen, M. U. R. Naidu, Y. S. N. Raju, and Naval Chandra. "Effect of NCB-02, Atorvastatin and Placebo on Endothelial Function, Oxidative Stress and Inflammatory Markers in Patients with Type 2 Diabetes Mellitus." *Drugs in R&D* 9 (2008): 2243–50. doi.org/10.216 5/00126839-200809040-00004.

Webb, Densie. "Anthocyanins." *Today's Dietician* 16, no. 3 (March 2014): 20. todaysdietitian.com/newarchives/030314p20.shtml.

Wongcharoen, Wanwarang, Sasivimon Jai-aue, Arintaya Phrommintikul, Weerachai Nawarawong, Surin Woragidpoonpol, Thitipong Tepsuwan, Apicahrd Sukonthasarn, Nattayaporn Apaijai, and Nipon Chattipakorn. "Effects of Curcuminoids on Frequency of Acute Myocardial Infarction after Coronary Artery Bypass Grafting." *American Journal of Cardiology* 110, no. 1 (July 2012): 40–44. doi.org/10.1016/j.amjcard.2012.02.043.

Yang, Tianxi, Jeffery Doherty, Bin Zhao, Amanda J. Kinchla, John M. Clark, and Lili He. "Effectiveness of Commercial and Homemade Washing Agents in Removing Pesticide Residues on and in Apples." *Journal of Agricultural and Food Chemistry* 65, no. 44 (2017): 9744–52. doi.org/10.1021/acs.jafc.7b03118.

Ye, Lingxiang, and Yuesheng Zhang. "Total Intracellular Accumulation Levels of Dietary Isothiocyanates Determine Their Activity in Elevation of Cellular Glutathione and Induction of Phase 2 Detoxification Enzymes." *Carcinogenesis* 22, no. 12 (December 2001): 1987–92. doi.org/10.1093/carcin/22.12.1987.

Zhang, Dong-wei, Min Fu, Si-Hua Gao, and Jun-Li Liu. "Curcumin and Diabetes: A Systematic Review." *Evidence-Based Complementary and Alternative Medicine* (2013). doi.org/10.1155/2013/636053.

Zunino, Susan J. "Type 2 Diabetes and Glycemic Response to Grapes or Grape Products." *Journal of Nutrition* 139, no. 9 (September 2009): 1794S–1800S. doi.org/10.3945/jn.109.107631.

INDEX

ACKNOWLEDGMENTS

I want to acknowledge the many physicians, scientists, researchers, health experts, health coaches, and juicing enthusiasts who have generously shared their many years of juicing and plant-based nutrition wisdom with the world. Because of their books, lectures, programs, and videos, I continue to implement and grow in my understanding of the power of juicing and a plant-based diet for remarkable health for my clients and myself.

I want to thank my husband, Doyle, for helping me test more than 350 juice blends and for providing feedback on the recipes for this book! His support and enthusiasm for juicing made all those hours in the kitchen and on my laptop a labor of love.

I also want to thank Callisto Media for making this book possible and my editors Rebecca Markley and Erika Sloan, who have been a joy to work with.

ABOUT THE AUTHOR

 **Stephanie Leach, HC, CJT,** is a certified health coach and certi-
fied juice therapist trained in the Juice Guru Method. Through
her coaching programs, website, and videos, she supports
individuals ready to harness the power of plants to achieve and
maintain a healthy weight and avoid or reverse chronic conditions. Based in Colorado, Stephanie enjoys juicing along with
gardening, mountain views, hiking, and wheeling. Learn more about Stephanie
on her website, StephanieLeach.com.